Top notch tv

VIDEO COURSE Fundamentals

TOP NOTCH TV

Joan Saslow ■ Allen Ascher

with *Top Notch Pop Songs and Karaoke*
by Rob Morsberger

PEARSON
Longman

Top Notch TV   Fundamentals
Video Course

Pearson Education, 10 Bank Street, White Plains, NY 10606

Staff credits: The people who made up the *Top Notch TV Fundamentals Video Course* team—representing editorial, production, design, and manufacturing—are Rhea Banker, Dave Dickey, Pamela Fishman, Patrice Fraccio, Ann France, Aliza Greenblatt, Ray Keating, Mike Kemper, Katherine Keyes, Jessica Miller-Smith, Michael Mone, and Martin Yu.

Text composition: TSI Graphics

Text font: Utopia

Cover credits: Ann France

Illustration credits: Ken Batelman, pp. 18, 19, 40, 41, 47 (top), 52; Scott Fray, pp. 49, 73; Mona Mark, p. 77; Sandy Nichols, p. 35; Dusan Petricic, pp. 41, 86, 90, 93, 96, 106 (top row and "graduate"); Phil Scheuer, pp. 55, 56 (bottom), 59 (bottom row), 95, 103, 106, 109 (bottom row); Don Stewart, p. 94; Neil Stewart, pp. 17, 19 (top), 20, 36, 56 (top); TSI Graphics, pp. 2, 48; Anna Veltfort pp. 9, 29, 55 (top, "watch TV"), 59 (top row), 100, 101, 103 (bottom).

Photo credits: All original photography by David Mager. Page 1 (chef) Alen Bolesta/Index Stock Imagery, (doctor) Jose Luis Pelaez, Inc/Corbis, (mail carrier) David Young-Wolff/PhotoEdit,(tour guide) Robert Brenner/PhotoEdit, (writer) Kim Steele/Getty Images, (artist) James P. Blair/Corbis, (lawyer) Royalty-Free/Corbis, (musician) Getty Images, (actor) Mark Richards/PhotoEdit, (architect) Royalty-Free/Corbis, (athlete) Jim Arbogast/Getty Images, (teacher) Jose Luis Pelaez, Inc/Corbis, (businessman/businesswoman) Michael S. Yamashita/Corbis, (manager) Tom McCarthy/PhotoEdit, (singer) Kevin Winter/Getty Images; p. 2 (architect) Royalty-Free/Corbis, (soccer players) AFP/Corbis; p. 12 (1) Lucy Nicholson/Reuters/Corbis, (2) AFP/Getty Images, (3) AP World Wide Photos, (4) Alexander Tamargo/Getty Images North America, (5) ArenaPal/Topham/The Image Works, (6) Getty Images; p. 17 (train station) Robert Frerck/Odyssey, (bank) Steve Dunwell/Getty Images, (newsstand) Jeff Greenberg/PhotoEdit, (bus station) John Elk III, (bookstore) Dave Bartruff/Corbis, (pharmacy) Bill Aron/ PhotoEdit, (park) Dave G. Houser/Corbis, (museum) Mimmo Jodice/Corbis; p. 22 (restaurant) Getty Images, (post office) Tom Carter/PhotoEdit, (travel agency) Bill Bachmann/PhotoEdit, (convenience store) Michael Newman/PhotoEdit, (taxi stand) Jeff Greenberg/PhotoEdit, (stadium) William Taufic/Corbis, (mall) Robert Frerck/ Odyssey, (airport) James Leynse/Corbis; p. 25 (pretty) Douglas Kirkland/Corbis, (handsome) Lisa O'Connor/ ZUMA/Corbis, (cute) Rick Gomez/Masterfile, (tall/short) Universal/The Kobal Collection, (old) Alpha Photo Press Agency Ltd./Globe Photos, (young) Corbis Sygma; p. 27 (top) Darama/Corbis; p. 33 (movie inset) Original Films/The Kobal Collection, (movie) Graham French/Masterfile, (play) Robbie Jack Photography, (concert) Stephanie Maze/Corbis, (party) Alamy Images, (game) AFP Corbis, (speech) Getty Images; p. 40 (shoe) Dorling Kindersley, (shirt) www.canz.biz, (sweater) Dorling Kindersley, (tie) www.canz.biz, (jacket) Andersen Ross/Getty Images, (skirt) FashionSyndicatePress.com, (dress) Carin Krasner/Corbis, (blouse & pants) Getty Images, (suit) FashionSyndicatePress.com; p. 41 (1) Lawrence Manning/Corbis, (3) Sandra Small Photography, (4) Courtesy of Museum of Textil y de la indumentaria; Ramon Manent/CORBIS, (5) iStockphoto; p. 73 (4) Luchschen/ Shutterstock, (5) OlgaLis/Shutterstock; p. 85 (1) Bill Bachmann/Mira.com, (2) Michael Keller/Corbis, (3) Getty Images, (4) Norbert Schaefer/Corbis, (5) Tim Kiusalaas/Corbis, (6) Alamy Images; p. 88 Dennis MacDonald/ PhotoEdit; p. 91 (red) Getty Images, (gray) Getty Images, (white) Getty Images; p. 94 (hands) Michael Keller/ Corbis; p. 106 (business) Jose Luis Pelaez, Inc./Corbis, (medicine) ATC Productions/Corbis; p. 107 (psychology) Jose Luis Pelaez, Inc./Corbis; p. 109 (golf) Comstock Images, (sailing)Royalty-Free/Corbis, (snorkeling) Royalty- Free/Corbis, (cruise) Gisela Damm/eStock Photo, (hiking) Pixtal/SuperStock, (skiing) Royalty-Free/Corbis; p. 111 (architecture) Peter Beck/Corbis, (education) Tom & Dee Ann McCarthy/Corbis, (mathematics) Jose Luis Pelaez, Inc./Corbis, (science) Andrew Douglas/Masterfile, (nursing) Getty Images, (engineering) Michael Keller/Corbis, (law) Billy E. Barnes/PhotoEdit.

ISBN 13: 978-0-13-205862-9
ISBN 10: 0-13-205860-X

Printed in the United States of America
1 2 3 4 5 6 7 8 9 10—RRD—12 11 10 09 08 07

Contents

(continued on page vi)

Scope and sequence of content and skills

UNIT	Social Language	Vocabulary	Grammar
1 **Nice to meet you.** *Page 1*	• Greetings and introductions	• Occupations	• Verb *be* • Singular and plural nouns • *A / an*
2 **Who's that?** *Page 9*	• Discuss nationalities and occupations • Get someone's address and phone number	• Numbers 0–20 • Relationships	• Possessive adjectives and nouns • *Be:* information questions with *Where* and *What*
3 **How do I get there?** *Page 17*	• Give and get directions	• Places in the community • Locations and directions	• The imperative • *There is*
4 **Who's this?** *Page 25*	• Talk about families	• Family members • Adjectives to describe people • Numbers 20–100	• *Very* and *so* • Questions with *Who* • Questions with *How old* • *Have / has:* affirmative statements
5 **You're late.** *Page 33*	• Talk about time and dates • Invite someone to an event	• Telling time • Events • Days of the week • Time expressions • Months of the year • Ordinal numbers	• *Be:* questions about time • Prepositions of time and place
6 **Do you like this blouse?** *Page 40*	• Express likes • Describe clothes	• Clothes • Colors and other descriptive adjectives • Verbs *want, have, need, like*	• *This / that / these / those* • The simple present tense
7 **Welcome to my new apartment.** *Page 47*	• Describe a home	• Houses and apartments • Rooms • Furniture and appliances	• *There is / there are, How many,* and *a lot of* • Prepositions of place

(continued on page viii)

About the Video Course

The *Top Notch TV Video Course* consists of four *Top Notch TV* videos and their corresponding Video Course Books. The course can be used in a number of ways:

- As a stand-alone video-based listening / speaking course that teaches key vocabulary, grammar, and social language
- As a video-plus-workbook supplement to accompany the *Top Notch* course*
- As a video-plus-workbook complement to any low-beginning to intermediate level English language course
- As a self-study or distance learning video-plus-workbook program

Top Notch TV

Top Notch TV consists of four graded videos designed for English language learning, ranging from true-beginner level to high-intermediate level. The videos contain:

- A hilarious TV-style sitcom (with a TV-style laugh track)
- Authentic, unrehearsed on-the-street interviews of speakers with a variety of accents
- Original Top Notch Pop Songs and Karaoke
- Optional closed captioning

Scope and Sequence

The scope and sequence chart on pages vii–viii indicates the language focus of each of the ten units of this Video Course Book. Answers to exercises and complete video scripts and *Top Notch Pop* song lyrics can be found at the end of this book.

Unit Organization

Each unit begins with a **Preview** section which presents and practices key language that will occur in the video. Then, activities for each video segment are organized into two sections: **View** and **Extend**.

View activities focus on comprehension and include "Sneak peeks" to build expectation for the topics of the sitcom episodes. View sections also include "Language in use" boxes pointing out interesting facts about spoken English.

Extend sections present additional topically related vocabulary and useful grammar to boost students' oral and written fluency. **Extend** activities have been designed either for self-study or for classroom interaction. They include writing practice as well as "Speaking options" for pair and group discussion.

A *Top Notch Pop* song section includes activities that practice the target language included in each *Top Notch Pop* song.

Note: Video Scripts, Lyrics, and Answer Keys are perforated and can be removed.

Top Notch is a complete four-level communicative course for adults and young adults. Together with *Summit 1* and *2*, it forms a six-level course with a full range of print and multimedia materials, including *Top Notch TV* and *Summit TV*.

About the authors

Joan Saslow

Ms. Saslow is co-author with Allen Ascher of the six-level award-winning adult course *Top Notch* and *Summit*. She was the series director of *True Colors*.

Joan Saslow is also author of a number of additional multi-level courses for adults: *Ready to Go*, *Workplace Plus*, and *Literacy Plus*, and of *English in Context: Reading Comprehension for Science and Technology*.

Ms. Saslow taught in Chile at the Binational Centers of Valparaíso and Viña del Mar and at the Catholic University of Valparaíso. In the United States, Ms. Saslow taught English as a Foreign Language to Japanese university students at Marymount College and workplace English at General Motors. She is a frequent speaker at gatherings of English teachers throughout the world. Ms. Saslow has an M.A. in French from the University of Wisconsin.

Allen Ascher

Allen Ascher, co-author with Joan Saslow of the six-level award-winning adult course *Top Notch* and *Summit*, is the author of the popular *Think about Editing: A Grammar Editing Guide for ESL Writers*. Mr. Ascher played a key publishing role in the creation of some of the most widely used materials for adults, including: *True Colors*, *NorthStar*, *Focus on Grammar*, *Global Links*, and *Ready to Go*.

Mr. Ascher has been a teacher and teacher-trainer in both China and the United States and was Academic Director of the International English Language Institute at Hunter College. He taught all skills and levels in the City University of New York and trained teachers in the certificate program at the New School. He has provided lively workshops at conferences throughout Asia, Latin America, North America, Europe, and the Middle East. Mr. Ascher has an M.A. in Applied Linguistics from Ohio University.

Meet the Top Notch TV stars

Mr. Evans, President of the
Top Notch Travel Agency

Bob, a travel agent

Cheryl, the office manager

Paul, a tour guide

Marie, the receptionist

Meet the on-the-street interviewees

(Any accents that depart from standard American English are labeled.)

Alexandra

Alvino

Angelique

Blanche / Herb

Catherine

Chris
(United Kingdom)

Christiane
(Austria)

Christine

Dan

Deepti
(India)

Elli

Emma

Ian

James
(Southern U.S.)

Jessica
(Germany)

Joe

Lisa

Lorayn

Maiko
(Japan)

Martin
(Taiwan)

Matt

Mauro

Natalie

Rita
(U.S. New York City)

Rob

San

Stephan
(Greece)

Vanessa
(U.S. New York City)

UNIT 1
Nice to meet you.

Social Language
• Greetings and introductions

Vocabulary
• Occupations

Grammar
• Verb *be*
• Singular and plural nouns
• *A / an*

Preview These exercises will help prepare you for the language in the video.

Expand your vocabulary

Occupations

a chef

a doctor

a mail carrier

a receptionist

a tour guide

a writer

an artist

a lawyer

a musician

an actor

an architect

an athlete

a teacher

a businessman /
a businesswoman

a manager

a singer

1

Match the pictures with the occupations. Write the letter on the line.

 a.  b.  c. 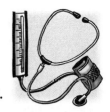 d.  e.

 f. 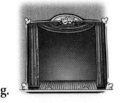 g.  h.  i.  j.

___ 1. chef   ___ 3. mail carrier   ___ 5. artist   ___ 7. doctor   ___ 9. tour guide

___ 2. actor   ___ 4. receptionist   ___ 6. singer   ___ 8. athlete   ___ 10. architect

---

Activate your grammar

A / an for singular nouns; -s for plural nouns

Singular nouns   **Plural nouns**

a receptionist   **an a**rchitect   athlete**s**

This is Bob. Bob is . . .

An actor!

 Circle a or an.

1. (ⓐ/ an) singer   6. (a / an) manager   11. (a / an) lawyer

2. (a / an) doctor   7. (a / an) artist   12. (a / an) businessman

3. (a / an) teacher   8. (a / an) engineer   13. (a / an) tour guide

4. (a / an) actor   9. (a / an) chef   14. (a / an) student

5. (a / an) writer   10. (a / an) musician   15. (a / an) athlete

SITCOM

running time — 1:29

It's a pleasure to meet you. I'm James Evans, president of Top Notch Travel.

 View Read each exercise and then watch the video for the answers.

A Match the person and the name.

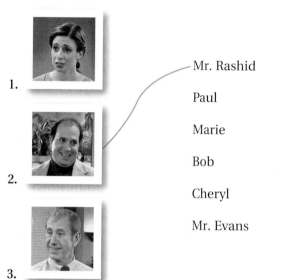

1.

2.

3.

Mr. Rashid

Paul

Marie

Bob

Cheryl

Mr. Evans

4.

5.

6.

B Check ☑ the greetings you hear in the video.

☐ Hello.
☐ Hi!
☐ How's it going?
☐ It's a pleasure to meet you.
☐ Good morning.

☐ Welcome to Top Notch.
☐ Nice to meet you.
☐ How are you?
☐ Glad to meet you.
☐ A pleasure.

C Mark each statement *T* (true) or *F* (false).

____ 1. Mr. Rashid is president of Top Notch Travel.

____ 2. Marie is the receptionist.

____ 3. Paul is a receptionist, too.

____ 4. Cheryl is the office manager.

____ 5. Bob is a chef.

____ 6. Bob is a doctor.

____ 7. Bob is a singer.

____ 8. Bob is an architect.

____ 9. Bob is an athlete.

Language in use

I'm the **mailman**.

mailman = mail carrier

3

Hi, I'm Paul.

Activate your grammar

Verb *be*: singular forms

Affirmative
I **am** [I'm] Marie.
You **are** [You're] an artist.
He **is** [He's] a receptionist.
She **is** [She's] Emily.

Negative
I **am not** [I'm not] Cheryl.
You **are not** [You're not / You aren't] a chef.
He **is not** [He's not / He isn't] an office manager.
She **is not** [She's not / She isn't] Laura.

D Complete each statement.

1. She's Marie. She's the _____.

2. _____ Cheryl. _____
   the _____.

3. Bob _____ a doctor. _____
   a singer. _____ an architect.

4. _____ Paul. _____ a
   _____.

5. Mr. Evans _____ the receptionist.
   _____ the president of Top Notch
   Travel.

6. Mr. Rashid _____ the office
   manager.

Activate your grammar

Be: plural forms

Affirmative	Negative
We **are** [We're] Paul and Marie.	We **are not** [We're not / We aren't] Bob and Cheryl.
You **are** [You're] at Top Notch Travel.	You **are not** [You're not / You aren't] at Tip Top Travel.
They **are** [They're] actors.	They **are not** [They're not / They aren't] chefs.

Be: yes / no questions and short answers

Yes / no questions	Short answers
Are you Bob?	Yes, I am. / No, I am not [I'm not].
Is she an office manager?	Yes, she is. / No, she is not [she's not / she isn't].
Is Paul a tour guide?	Yes, he is. / No, he is not [he's not / he isn't].
Are you doctors?	Yes, we are. / No, we are not [we're not / we aren't].
Are they Cheryl and Marie?	Yes, they are. / No, they are not [they're not / they aren't].

E Write a question for each answer.

1. _____?

   Yes. I'm Bob.

2. _____?

   No. I'm not an office manager.

3. _____?

   No. Mr. Evans is not a tour guide. He's the president of Top Notch Travel.

4. _____?

   No. They're not Bob and Mr. Evans. They're Paul and Mr. Rashid.

F Write one *yes / no* question and one short answer about each of the people at Top Notch Travel.

> **1. Bob:** Is Bob a doctor?
> No, he's not.

1. Bob:	**4. Marie:**
2. Paul:	**5. Mr. Evans:**
3. Cheryl:	**6. Mr. Rashid:**

Speaking option: **Ask a classmate your questions.**

Write sentences introducing the class to the people at Top Notch Travel.

This is Mr. Evans. He's the president of Top Notch Travel.

_____

_____

_____

_____

_____

_____

_____

_____

_____

_____

_____

_____

Speaking option: Introduce the people at Top Notch Travel to your classmates. Use your sentences and the pictures.

ON-THE-STREET INTERVIEWS

Hi. How are you today?

running time — 1:09

View Read each exercise and then watch the video for the answers.

A Answer the questions about the people.

1. Is he a teacher?

_____.

2. Is she a teacher?

_____.

3. Is she a businesswoman?

_____.

4. Is she a doctor?

_____.

B Read the interviewer's question or statement. Choose the correct response, according to what you hear in the video.

1.

How are you today?

a. I'm fine.
b. Good. How are you?
c. Not too good.

2.
What do you do?

a. I'm a teacher.
b. I work in a hotel.
c. I'm an architect.

3.

What's your name?

a. My name's Christiane.
b. I'm Christiane.
c. Christiane.

4.

Take care. Have a nice day.

a. You take care as well.
b. You, too.
c. You as well. Bye-bye.

Expand your vocabulary

Greetings and introductions

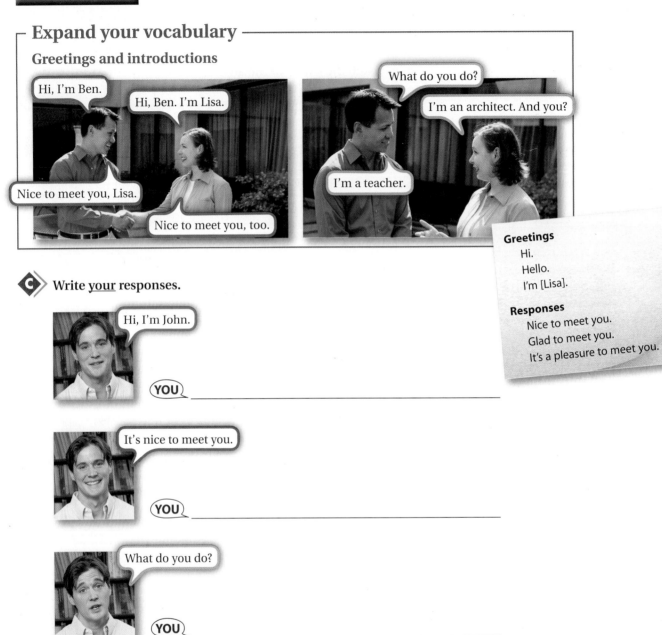

Hi, I'm Ben.

Hi, Ben. I'm Lisa.

Nice to meet you, Lisa.

Nice to meet you, too.

What do you do?

I'm an architect. And you?

I'm a teacher.

Greetings
Hi.
Hello.
I'm [Lisa].

Responses
Nice to meet you.
Glad to meet you.
It's a pleasure to meet you.

C Write <u>your</u> responses.

Hi, I'm John.

YOU _____

It's nice to meet you.

YOU _____

What do you do?

YOU _____

Speaking option: **Meet and greet your classmates.**

UNIT 2
Who's that?

Social Language
- Discuss nationalities and occupations
- Get someone's address and phone number

Vocabulary
- Numbers 0–20
- Relationships

Grammar
- Possessive adjectives and nouns
- *Be*: information questions with *Where* and *What*

Preview These exercises will help prepare you for the language in the video.

That's Alan Reese. He's **our** lawyer.

Activate your grammar

Possessive adjectives and nouns

Possessive adjectives
- Dr. Jones is **my** doctor.
- Lynne is **his** student.
- Paul is not **their** teacher.

Possessive nouns
- Mr. Smith is **Laura's** teacher.
- Ms. Gray is **Jason's** lawyer.
- **Nancy and Clark's** boss is Mr. Bello.

Subject pronouns		Possessive adjectives
I	→	my
you	→	your
he	→	his
she	→	her
we	→	our
they	→	their

 A Look at the pictures and complete each statement about the relationships. Use a possessive noun and then a possessive adjective.

David   Rick

1. David is ___Rick's___ classmate.
   _{Rick}

   David is ___his___ classmate.
   _{he}

Judy   Vivian

2. Judy is _____ friend.
   _{Vivian}

   Judy is _____ friend.
   _{she}

Pam   Ken   Rob

3. Rob is _____ neighbor.
   _{Pam and Ken}

   Rob is _____ neighbor.
   _{they}

Ann   Joan

4. Ann is _____ boss.
   _{Joan}

   Ann is _____ boss.
   _{she}

Andrew

Henry

5. Henry is _____ colleague.
   _{Andrew}

   Henry is _____ colleague.
   _{he}

SITCOM

running time — 1:48

Who's that?

View Read each exercise and then watch the video for the answers.

 A Match each person with an occupation or relationship.

___ 1. Arturo Montoya   a. writer

___ 2. David Ducain   b. doctor

___ 3. Mr. Evans   c. artist

___ 4. Clark Thomas   d. lawyer

___ 5. Jeff Davis   e. musician

___ 6. Alan Reese   f. boss

B Complete the scripts, according to what they say in the video.

Language in use

Hey, guys!

Hey, guys (very informal) = Hello.

That's _____ David Ducain.
He's _____ from France.

1.

That's Arturo Montoya. He's
_____.
He's _____ from Mexico.

2.

No. That's Jeff Davis. He's
_____.

No. That's Alan Reese. He's _____.

That's _____ Alan Reese.

Oh! It's Clark Thomas from England. He's _____.

3.

That's Mr. Evans. He's _____.

_____ Mr. Evans.

4.

C **Complete each sentence with *is, isn't, are,* or *aren't.***

1. Marie, Paul, and Bob _____ Cheryl's colleagues.

2. Bob _____ Cheryl's boss.

3. Mr. Evans _____ Bob's boss.

4. David Ducain _____ Bob's friend.

5. David Ducain _____ Paul's friend.

6. Jeff Davis and Alan Reese _____ Paul's classmates.

7. Mr. Montoya _____ Mr. Evans's neighbor.

8. Bob and Paul _____ colleagues.

9. Clark Thomas _____ from France.

 These exercises will help improve your fluency.

 Write about your relationships.

Keith Brown is my neighbor.

Relationships
friend
classmate
neighbor
colleague
boss

 Speaking option: **Tell a classmate about your relationships.**

 Write about the people.

1.

Name: Maria Sharapova
Occupation: athlete
Country: Russia

This is Maria Sharapova. She's an athlete.
She's from Russia.

2.
Name: Nobu Matsuhisa
Occupation: chef
Country: Japan

_____
_____

3.

Name: Frank Gehry
Occupation: architect
Country: Canada

_____
_____

4.

Name: Paulina Rubio
Occupation: singer
Country: Mexico

_____
_____

5.

Name: Martha Argerich
Occupation: musician
Country: Argentina

_____
_____

6.

Name: Djimon Hounsou
Occupation: actor
Country: Benin

_____
_____

 Speaking option: **With a classmate, take turns talking about the people.**

ON-THE-STREET INTERVIEWS

running time — 1:05

Where are you from?

View Read each exercise and then watch the video for the answers.

A Complete the scripts, according to what they say in the video.

1. Where are you from?

_____ Oklahoma.

_____ Bristol in England.

2. And _____ the United States?

_____.

B Complete the information for each person.

1. First name: _____
   Last name: _____
   Country: <u>India</u> _____

2. First name: <u>Lisa</u> _____
   Phone number: _____

3. First name: <u>Matt</u> _____
   Address: _____ Concord Square

4. First name: <u>Elli</u> _____
   Last name: _____
   E-mail address: _____

5. First name: <u>Ian</u> _____
   Cell-phone number: _____

Numbers 0–20

0 zero	7 seven	14 fourteen
1 one	8 eight	15 fifteen
2 two	9 nine	16 sixteen
3 three	10 ten	17 seventeen
4 four	11 eleven	18 eighteen
5 five	12 twelve	19 nineteen
6 six	13 thirteen	20 twenty

Language in use

Yep.

Yep [or **Yup**] (very informal) = Yes.

Extend

These exercises will help improve your fluency.

C Circle the correct word to complete each sentence.

1. (She's / Her / He's / His) from Oklahoma.

2. (She's / Her / He's / His) from England.

3. (She's / Her / He's / His) first name is Matt.

4. (She's / Her / He's / His) from India.

5. (She's / Her / He's / His) first name is Elli.

Activate your grammar

Be: information questions with *Where* and *What*

Questions	Answers
Where's she from?	Canada.
Where are your friends from?	Tokyo.
What's your last name?	Smith.
What's his address?	26 Singer Street.
What's his first name?	Bob.
What's your e-mail address?	pat@annex.com.
What's their phone number?	555-9087.

Where is → **Where's**
What is → **What's**

In e-mail addresses, say
*pat **at** annex **dot** com*

In phone numbers, say *oh* for *zero*:
five-five-five-nine-**oh**-eight-seven

D Write a question for each answer.

1. _____ ?

   I'm from Japan.

2. _____ ?

   My name's Nicole.

3. _____ ?

   It's 555-67-53-24.

4. _____ ?

   It's hank@kiwi.nz.

5. _____ ?

   My neighbors are from Chile.

6. _____ ?

   It's 76 Artist Street.

E Answer the questions about yourself.

1. What's your name?

   _____

2. How do you spell that?

   _____

3. What city are you from?

   _____

4. What's your cell-phone number?

   _____

5. And your address?

   _____

6. What's your e-mail address?

   _____

Speaking option: Ask your classmates the questions. Write the information below.

name	city	cell phone	address	e-mail
John Vogos	Los Angeles	310-555-8970	15 Third Street	jvogus@newnet.com

	name	city	cell phone	address	e-mail
1.					
2.					
3.					
4.					
5.					

TOP NOTCH POP SONG   Excuse Me, Please

running time — 1:48

A ▷ **Listen to the song "Excuse Me, Please." Then listen again without looking at the screen and complete the questions you hear in the lyrics.**

Excuse me—please excuse me. What's your _____? What's your _____?

1.   2.

I would love to get to know you, and I hope you feel the same.

I'll give you my e-mail address. Write to me at my dot-com.

You can send a note in English so I'll know who it came from.

Excuse me—please excuse me. Was that _____?

3.

Well, I think the class is starting, and I don't want to be late.

But it's really nice to meet you. I'll be seeing you again.

Just call me on my cell phone when you're looking for a friend.

Excuse me—please excuse me. What's _____ number? What's _____ name?

4.   5.

I would love to get to know you, and I hope you feel the same.

So welcome to the classroom. There's a seat right over there.

I'm sorry, but you're sitting in our teacher's favorite chair!

Excuse me—please excuse me. _____ your number? _____ your name?

6.   7.

B ▷ **Listen again. Complete the following statements.**

1. The singer wants the new classmate to write him at his _____.

2. The singer wants the new classmate to call him on his _____.

C ▷ **Answer these questions.**

1. What two things does the singer ask the new classmate?

   a. _____

   b. _____

2. Where do you think they are?

   _____

UNIT 3
How do I get there?

Social Language
• Give and get directions

Vocabulary
• Places in the community
• Locations and directions

Grammar
• The imperative
• *There is*

Preview These exercises will help prepare you for the language in the video.

Expand your vocabulary

Places in the community

a train station

a bank

a newsstand

a bus station

a bookstore

a pharmacy

a park

a museum

Expand your vocabulary

Locations and directions

Around the corner . . .

across the street

around the corner

down the street

on the left

on the right

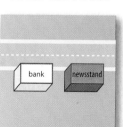
next to the bank

17

Answer each question. Use the pictures on page 17.

1. Where's the bank? _It's next to the newsstand._
2. Where's the museum? _Down the street_
3. Where's the bus station? _on the right_
4. Where's the bookstore? _around the corner_
5. Where's the pharmacy? _on the left_
6. Where's the train station? _across the street_

Activate your grammar

The imperative

Use imperatives to give directions.

 Take the train to the museum.

 Don't take the bus.

| **Affirmative** | | | **Negative** | | |

Take a taxi.   Drive.   Walk.   Don't take a taxi.   Don't drive.   Don't walk.

Complete each statement. Use the imperative.

1. _____Take_____ the bus. _____Don't walk_____.

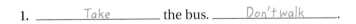

2. _____. _____ the train.

3. _____ a taxi. _____ the bus.

4. _____ the train. _____.

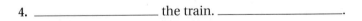

5. _____. _____.

Expand your vocabulary

Directions with the imperative

Turn right.
OR: Turn right at the corner.

Turn left.
OR: Turn left at the corner.

Go straight.

Park Avenue

Main Street

**Go to the corner of Main
Street and Park Avenue.**

**Go two blocks and
turn left.**

C Look at the map and complete the conversations.

1. A: Where's the train station?
   B: ____Go____ straight.
   It's on the right.

2. A: How do I get to the bus
   station?
   B: ____Turn____ left.
   ____Go____ one block.
   It's around the corner.

3. A: How do I get to the museum?
   B: ____Go to the corner____ of
   Bank Street and A Street. It's
   on the left.

4. A: Is there a newsstand around here?
   B: Yes. Go to B Street and ____turn left____ at the corner. Go ____one____ block to New Street.
   ____Turn right____ at the corner. It's on the left.

5. A: How do I get to the park?
   B: Go ____2____ blocks and turn ____right____. It's on the left.

Newsstand

Taft Museum

Central
Park

NEW STREET

Bus Station

Central
Train Station

A STREET

BANK STREET

B STREET

C STREET

SITCOM

running time — 1:51

Sneak peek

Excuse me. How do I get to the Red Café?

View Read each exercise and then watch the video for the answers.

A Check ☑ the locations you hear.

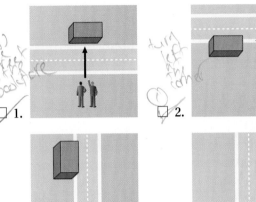

[handwritten: across the street to the bookstore]

☑ 1.

[handwritten: turn left at the corner]

☑ 2.

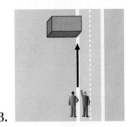

☐ 3.

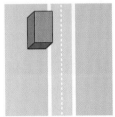

☐ 4.

☐ 5.

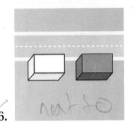

☑ 6. *[handwritten: next to]*

B Correct the directions, according to what Mr. Evans says in the video.

1. Go to the corner and turn right. *[handwritten: left]*

_____

2. Go three blocks and turn left. *[handwritten: right]*

_____

3. Take the train. *[handwritten: Don't]*

_____

4. Go through the park. *[handwritten: station]*

_____

Language in use

Got it?

Got it? (very informal) = Do you understand?

C Choose the correct word or phrase to complete each statement.

1. The train station is _____.
   a. across the street   (b.) around the corner   c. on the left

2. The bookstore is _____.
   (a.) across the street   b. around the corner   c. on the left

3. The Red Café is next to the _____.
   a. bookstore   (b.) pharmacy   c. train station

D Number the directions in the correct order.

Let's do it again.

__8__ Across the street.

__7__ Through the station.

__11__ Red Café!

__5__ Around the corner.

__3__ Two blocks.

__10__ Pharmacy.

__4__ Right.

__2__ Left.

__6__ Don't take the train!

__1__ Corner.

__9__ Bookstore.

E Write the directions to the Red Café.

Go to the corner and . . .

These exercises will help improve your fluency.

Expand your vocabulary

More places in the community

a restaurant

a post office

a travel agency

a convenience store

a taxi stand

a stadium

a mall

an airport

F Write directions to a place near your class.

Place:	
Directions:	

 Speaking option: Give a partner your directions. Your partner writes them on a separate sheet of paper.

ON-THE-STREET
INTERVIEWS
running time — 1:05

Is there a bank near here?

 View Read each exercise and then watch the video for the answers.

A Match each person with the question he or she answers.

 a.　 b.　 c.　 d.　 e.

___ 1. "Tell me, is there a bank near here?"

_c_ 2. "Excuse me. Is there a newsstand nearby?"

_A_ 3. "Do you know if there's a restaurant nearby?"

_e_ 4. "Is there a taxi stand nearby?"

___ 5. "Could you tell me how to get to the train station?"

 B Choose the correct answers, according to what they say in the video.

1. How many banks are nearby?
   a. One.　　b. Two.　　(c.) Three.

2. How do you get to the newsstand?
   (a.) Go down the street. Make a right. It's on the right.
   b. Go down the street. Make a left. It's on the left.
   c. Go down the street. Make a right. It's around the corner.

3. Where's the restaurant?
   a. On the corner of Tavern Street and Green Street.
   (b.) In the park.
   c. Across the street.

4. Where is the taxi stand?
   a. Down the street.
   b. Next to the bookstore.
   (c.) There isn't a taxi stand nearby.

5. How do you get to the train station?
   (a.) Walk down the street for thirty blocks.
   b. Walk down the street for thirteen blocks.
   c. Walk down the street for three blocks.

Language in use

Make a right, go one block . . .

Make a right (informal) = Turn right.

Extend These exercises will help improve your fluency.

Activate your grammar

Contractions
There is → **There's**
There is not → **There isn't**
OR: **There's not**

There is

Questions
　Is there a bookstore near here?
　Is there a bank near here?
　Is there a pharmacy on Smith Street?

Answers
　Yes. **There's** a bookstore across the street.
　Yes, there is. / No, there's not.
　Yes, there is. / No, there's not.

Be careful!
Yes, there is.
NOT ~~Yes, there's.~~

 C Answer the interviewer's questions about places in your community.

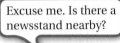 Excuse me. Is there a newsstand nearby?

Yes, there is. There's one right down the street . . .

1. Tell me, is there a bank near here?

_____

2. Excuse me. Is there a newsstand nearby?

_____

3. Do you know if there's a restaurant nearby?

_____

4. Is there a taxi stand nearby?

_____

　Speaking option: Ask your classmates the questions.

D Write about the places in your community.

There's a newsstand across from . . .

　Speaking option: With a classmate, discuss places in the community.

UNIT 4
Who's this?

Social Language
• Talk about families

Vocabulary
• Family members
• Adjectives to describe people
• Numbers 20–100

Grammar
• *Very* and *so*
• Questions with *Who*
• Questions with *How old*
• *Have / has*: affirmative statements

Preview These exercises will help prepare you for the language in the video.

Expand your vocabulary

Family members

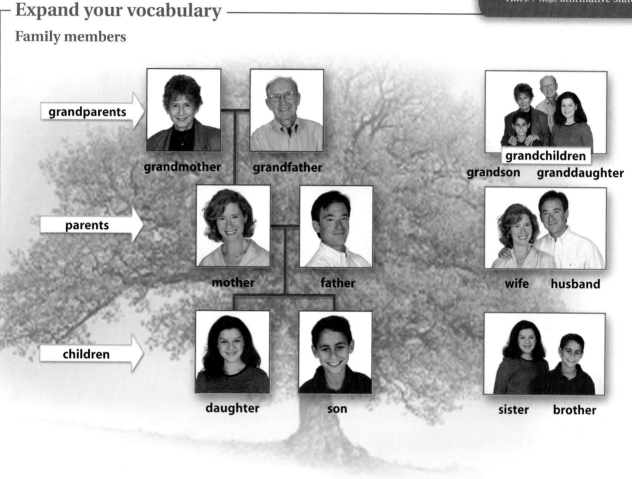

grandparents → grandmother   grandfather

grandchildren
grandson   granddaughter

parents → mother   father

wife   husband

children → daughter   son

sister   brother

Expand your vocabulary

Adjectives to describe people

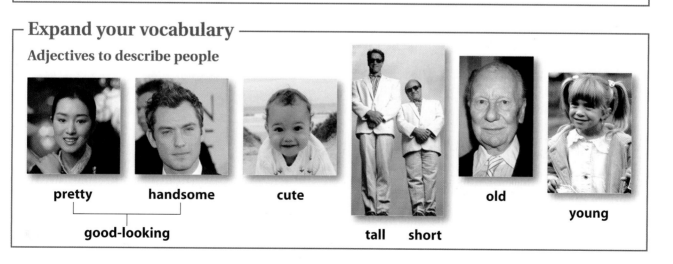

pretty   handsome   cute   old   young

good-looking   tall   short

25

Complete the sentences about the people in the photos. Choose the best answers.

1. Brian's sister is so _____!
   a. old   b. pretty   c. short

2. Her husband is so _____!
   a. pretty   b. short   c. handsome

3. My grandparents are very _____.
   a. old   b. tall   c. handsome

4. Her brother is very _____.
   a. tall   b. short   c. old

> The adverbs *so* and *very* make adjectives stronger.
> His daughter is **so** cute!
> She's **very** tall.

┌─ **Activate your grammar** ─────────

Be: questions with Who

Use *Who* to ask about people.
Who is he?	He's my son.
Who are they?	They're my sisters.
Who are Tim and Matt?	They're my brothers.

Who's this?

Contraction
Who is → Who's

Be careful!
Who are
NOT ~~Who're~~

B Look at the picture. Write questions with *Who* and the correct name.

Mark   Judy   Ann   Joe

Katie   Eric

1. A: <u>Who is Ann</u>?
    B: She's Joe's wife.

2. A: _____?
    B: They're Katie's grandparents.

3. A: _____?
    B: He's Joe's grandson.

4. A: _____?
    B: He's Judy's husband.

5. A: _____?
    B: She's Judy's daughter.

6. A: _____?
    B: They're Joe and Ann's grandchildren.

Activate your grammar

How old is he?

Be: questions with *How old*

How old is she?	She's twenty-seven years old.
How old is your mother?	She's fifty-seven.
How old are they?	Jack is five and Tracy is ten.

C Complete the conversations.

1. A: _____ your grandfather?
    B: He's eighty-three.

2. A: _____ Nancy's grandchildren?
    B: Ken _____ nine and Cindy
       _____ eleven.

3. A: _____ your daughter?
    B: _____ fifteen years old.

4. A: _____?
    B: Jack's wife is thirty-six.

5. A: _____?
    B: My mother _____ forty-seven and my father _____ fifty-one.

6. A: _____ his children?
    B: Twenty-two and twenty-four.

Numbers 20–100

20 twenty	...	
21 twenty-one	30 thirty	60 sixty
22 twenty-two	31 thirty-one	70 seventy
23 twenty-three	...	80 eighty
24 twenty-four	40 forty	90 ninety
25 twenty-five	50 fifty	100 one hundred

SITCOM

running time — 2:07

Who's this short old woman?

That is not a short old woman.

View Read each exercise and then watch the video for the answers.

 A Check ☑ Cheryl's family members that Marie and Cheryl talk about.

Is this your family?

Yes.

☐ her brother   ☐ her mother
☐ her brother's wife   ☐ her grandfather
☐ her sister   ☐ her sister's husband
☐ her sister's daughter   ☐ her father
☐ her grandmother   ☐ her sister's son

B Mark each statement *T* (true) or *F* (false). Correct each false statement.

_____ 1. Cheryl's brother is a ~~writer~~. *doctor*

_____ 2. Her brother is twenty-five.

_____ 3. Her mother is sixty-eight.

_____ 4. Her sister is an architect.

_____ 5. Her sister's son is a student.

_____ 6. The short old woman in the photo is Cheryl.

Language in use

He's a university student.

He's so cute!

cute (informal) = handsome or pretty

C Choose the correct answer to each question about Cheryl's family.

1. Who's thirty-four?
   a. Her brother.   b. Her sister.   c. Her mother.

2. Who's a student?
   a. Her brother's son.   b. Her sister's son.   c. Her brother.

3. Who's fifty-eight?
   a. Her brother.   b. Her sister.   c. Her mother.

4. Who's so young?
   a. Her brother's son.   b. Her sister's son.   c. Her sister.

5. Who's very pretty?
   a. Her brother's wife.   b. Her sister's husband.   c. Her mother.

D How does Marie describe Cheryl's family members? Complete the statements.

1. Her brother: "He's so _____."

2. Her brother's wife: "She's very _____."

3. Her mother: "But she's so _____."

4. Her sister's son: "He's so _____!"

Extend These exercises will help improve your fluency.

┌─ **Activate your grammar** ─────────────────────────────────────┐

Have / has: affirmative statements

I
You
We
They
} **have** a son.

He
She
} **has** three daughters.

I **have** one brother and one sister.   She **has** three daughters.

└───┘

E Complete the conversations. Use *have, has, is,* or *are.*

1. A: Tell me about your family.
   B: Well, I _____ one brother and one sister.
   A: How old _____ they?
   B: My brother _____ twenty-two. And my sister _____ only sixteen.

2. A: Tell me about your mother's family.
   B: My mother _____ one brother and one sister. They _____ both teachers.
   A: What about children?
   B: My mother's brother _____ two daughters. But her sister _____ no children.

3. A: Tell me about your brother. How old _____ he?
   B: He _____ twenty-eight. He _____ a photographer.
   A: _____ he handsome?
   B: Yes, he _____.

F Write a short paragraph describing Cheryl's family.

> Cheryl has a brother and a sister. Her brother is a doctor, and he's very handsome.

Speaking option: With a partner, take turns describing Cheryl's family.

ON-THE-STREET INTERVIEWS

running time — 1:06

Do you have any children?

 View Read each exercise and then watch the video for the answers.

A Choose the correct word or phrase to complete each statement.

1. Rita has _____.
   a. a son and a daughter
   b. two sons and one daughter
   c. one son and two daughters

2. Chris has _____.
   a. a brother
   b. a sister
   c. two sisters

3. Mauro has _____.
   a. two sons
   b. two daughters
   c. a son and a daughter

4. Maiko has _____.
   a. a brother
   b. a sister
   c. a brother and a sister

B Complete the scripts, according to what they say in the video.

1.

_____ that in the picture in your left hand?

Could you tell me how old your _____ are?

_____ two girls and a boy.

Yes. My oldest boy is _____, soon to be _____. The second one, who is a girl, is _____. And my baby is _____.

2.

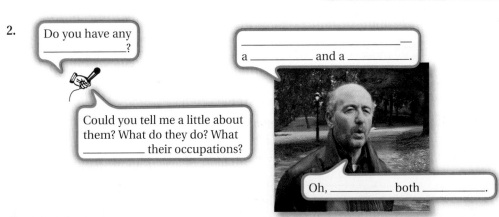

Do you have any _____?

Could you tell me a little about them? What do they do? What _____ their occupations?

_____ — a _____ and a _____.

Oh, _____ both _____.

◀C▶ **Mark each statement *T* (true), *F* (false), or *NI* (no information).**

_____ 1. Rita's son is forty.

_____ 2. Rita has three children.

_____ 3. Mauro's son is twenty-three.

_____ 4. Mauro's daughter is a student.

_____ 5. Chris's sister is twenty-six.

_____ 6. Maiko's brother is short and handsome.

Language in use

My oldest **boy** is . . . The second one, who is a **girl**, is . . . And my **baby** is . . .

a **boy** (informal) = son
a **girl** (informal) = daughter
the **baby** (informal) = youngest son or daughter

Extend   These exercises will help improve your fluency.

◀D▶ **Write about their families.**

Rita

1. <u>Rita has a son and two daughters.</u>
   <u>Her son is . . .</u>
   _____

Mauro

2. _____
   _____
   _____

Chris

3. _____
   _____
   _____

Maiko

4. _____
   _____
   _____

🗣 **Speaking option: With a partner, take turns talking about Rita's, Mauro's, Chris's, and Maiko's families.**

◀E▶ **What about you? On a separate sheet of paper, write about your family.**

🗣 **Speaking option: Tell your class about your family.**

31

TOP NOTCH POP SONG   Tell Me All about It

running time — 3:02

A Listen to the song. Then listen again and check ☑ the occupations you hear.

☐ doctor   ☐ lawyer   ☐ student   ☐ pilot
☐ engineer   ☐ actor   ☐ artist   ☐ teacher

B Listen again and write the names of the family members you hear.

1. _____*father*_____

2. _____

3. _____

4. _____

C Mark each statement *T* (true) or *F* (false), according to the information in the song.

_____ 1. Her father is a lawyer.

_____ 2. Her mother is a lawyer.

_____ 3. Her father is not tall.

_____ 4. Her brother and sister are artists.

_____ 5. Her sister is twenty-three.

_____ 6. He doesn't have a sister.

_____ 7. His parents are both teachers.

D Answer the questions. Listen again if necessary.

1. Is her father a doctor? _____

2. Is her mother a doctor or a lawyer? _____

3. How old is her brother? _____

4. What's his occupation? _____

5. Is her brother or her sister an artist? _____

6. How many brothers and sisters does he have? _____

7. What color are his mother's eyes? _____

UNIT 5
You're late.

Social Language
• Talk about time and dates
• Invite someone to an event

Vocabulary
• Telling time
• Events
• Days of the week
• Time expressions
• Months of the year
• Ordinal numbers

Grammar
• *Be:* questions about time
• Prepositions of time and place

Preview These exercises will help prepare you for the language in the video.

Expand your vocabulary

What time is it?

It's one o'clock.

It's one fifteen. OR:
It's a quarter after one.

It's one twenty. OR:
It's twenty after one.

It's one thirty. OR:
It's half past one.

It's one forty. OR:
It's twenty to two.

It's one forty-five. OR:
It's a quarter to two.

It's noon.

It's midnight.

24:00 → 11:59 = A.M.
12:00 → 23:59 = P.M.

Say *eight* A.M. **or** *eight* P.M.

Expand your vocabulary

Events

a movie

a play

a concert

a party

a game

a speech (OR: a talk)

33

Expand your vocabulary

Days of the week

A WEEK

WEEKDAYS   THE WEEKEND

Monday	Tuesday	Wednesday	Thursday	Friday	Saturday	Sunday

A Look at the newspaper. Then mark each statement *T* (true) or *F* (false).

_____ 1. The baseball game is at Gleason Field.

_____ 2. *No More Tears* is a play.

_____ 3. The Lions and the Tigers are baseball teams.

_____ 4. *No Dinner for Sam* is at 8:30.

_____ 5. *Dramarama* is a play.

_____ 6. The City Center's phone number is 566-32-659.

_____ 7. The tennis game is at 6:00.

_____ 8. *A Light in the Kitchen* is at 8:30 on Friday.

_____ 9. *Captain Bob, Marine Explorer* is the name of a movie.

_____ 10. *Love in the Afternoon* is at midnight on Friday.

This week's entertainment
Friday, April 6th

Movies **The Cine-Star (566-32-659)**
Space Raiders 7:00 9:00 12:00
Love in the Afternoon 8:30 10:30
    Midnight show Saturday only
Captain Bob, Marine Explorer 5:15 7:15

The City Center (231-88-901)
My Life as an Actress 6:00 8:45
No More Tears 7:45 9:15
In the Last War 9:00 11:45

Plays **The Dramarama (745-18-092)**
A Light in the Kitchen 8:00 (Friday)
                8:30 (Saturday)

The Berkley Theater (923-00-321)
    www.berkleytheater.com
No Dinner for Sam 8:30

The Hayes Theater (912-34-561)
Late in the Game 8:15

Games **Thomson Stadium:** Tennis Finals 6:00
Gleason Field: Baseball
    (Lions vs. Tigers) 7:30

Activate your grammar

Be: questions about time

Questions	Answers
What time is it?	Two o'clock.
What time is the baseball game?	8:00.
When is the movie?	Five thirty.
What day is the play?	Tuesday.

What time is it?

Contractions
What time is → What time**'s**
When is → When**'s**

Be careful!
What time's the class?
NOT What time's ~~it~~?

B Look at the newspaper again. Write short answers to the questions about the events.

1. When is *No More Tears*? _7:45 and 9:15_____

2. What days is *A Light in the Kitchen* at the Dramarama Theater? _____

3. What time is the play *No Dinner for Sam*? _____

Sneak peek

A baseball game! That sounds great!

 Read each exercise and then watch the video for the answers.

A Write the five events Cheryl and Bob discuss.

1. a _____   3. a _____   5. a _____

2. a _____   4. a _____

Time expressions

B Mark each statement *T* (true) or *F* (false). Correct each false statement.

_____ 1. Bob is ~~five~~ *two* minutes late.

_____ 2. Cheryl's birthday is on Saturday.

_____ 3. Bob's birthday is on Sunday.

_____ 4. There's a great French play at the Avalon.

_____ 5. There's a baseball game on Saturday.

_____ 6. *Life Is a Dream* is a movie.

_____ 7. The Tigers and the Giants are two baseball teams.

_____ 8. There's no Mozart concert on Saturday.

_____ 9. There's a concert at 7:30.

_____ 10. Ellen Lee's talk is at the University.

early

on time

late

C Complete each statement with *Cheryl, Bob,* or *Cheryl and Bob.*

1. _____ are in a restaurant.

2. _____'s birthday is on Saturday.

3. _____ says that _____ is late for their date.

4. _____ says it's five to six.

5. _____ says it's two minutes after six.

6. _____ wants to see a play, but _____ wants to see a baseball game.

7. _____ decide to go to a baseball game.

D Answer each question, according to the video.

1. What time is it? _____

2. Is Bob late? _____

3. When is Bob's birthday? _____

4. Is there a Brazilian movie at the Avalon? _____

5. When is the baseball game? _____

6. Where is the play? _____

7. What's the name of the play? _____

8. What time's the play? _____

9. What's at half past seven? _____

E Complete the scripts, according to what they say in the video.

1. **Cheryl:** You're _____.
   Bob: _____?
   Cheryl: Two minutes _____.

2. **Cheryl:** So for your birthday on _____,
   _____ a great French _____ at the Avalon.
   Bob: _____ a baseball _____ on
   _____ night.
   Cheryl: Or _____ a _____ at the Arts
   Center at _____. *Life Is a Dream.*

3. **Cheryl:** Oh, look! _____ a Mozart
   _____ on Saturday. Would you
   like to go?
   Bob: _____?

4. **Bob:** The ball game's at _____.
   Cheryl: Oh, wow! _____ by the
   writer Ellen Lee at the University on . . .
   Bob: On _____ night.

Activate your grammar

Prepositions of time and place

Time

at	on	in
at 2:30	on May 11th	in August
at noon	on Thursday	in the morning
at midnight	on the weekend	in the afternoon
at night	on a weekday	in the evening

Place

at	on	in OR at
at the movies	on Green Street	in / at the theater
at the concert	on the right	in / at the stadium
at the game	on the corner	in / at the park
at home		in / at the mall
at work		in / at the restaurant
at school		

Months of the year

January	April	July	October
February	May	August	November
March	June	September	December

Ordinal numbers

1st	first	17th	seventeenth
2nd	second	18th	eighteenth
3rd	third	19th	nineteenth
4th	fourth	20th	twentieth
5th	fifth	21st	twenty-first
6th	sixth	22nd	twenty-second
7th	seventh	23rd	twenty-third
8th	eighth	24th	twenty-fourth
9th	ninth	25th	twenty-fifth
10th	tenth	26th	twenty-sixth
11th	eleventh	27th	twenty-seventh
12th	twelfth	28th	twenty-eighth
13th	thirteenth	29th	twenty-ninth
14th	fourteenth	30th	thirtieth
15th	fifteenth	31st	thirty-first
16th	sixteenth		

F Complete the sentences with prepositions.

1. The play is _____ Wednesday _____ 8:30 _____ night.

2. The concert is _____ September 15th _____ 7:30 P.M. _____ the park.

3. There's a party _____ school _____ 2:30 _____ the afternoon _____ Friday.

4. The baseball game is _____ April _____ the Central Stadium _____ Bank Street.

5. There's a speech _____ work _____ 10:00 _____ the morning _____ July 22nd.

G On a separate sheet of paper, write a video script between two people deciding what to do on the weekend. Use the newspaper ads.

Weekend Entertainment

Friday, August 3 - Sunday, August 5

MOVIES

The Green Bottle
Friday 9:00 p.m.
Saturday and Sunday
10:00 p.m.
The Movietime Theater

At the Beach
Friday and Saturday
2:00, 4:00, 6:00, 8:00
Fleet Street Cinema

PLAYS

Home for the Holidays
Friday night 8:00
Saturday night 8:30
Sunday closed
The Classic Theater

Singing My Song
Saturday only,
7:45 p.m.
The Bellevue

SPORTS

Baseball
Venezuela vs. Korea
7:30 p.m.
City Stadium

A: "Singing My Song" is at the Bellevue. Would you like to go?
B: What time?

Speaking option: Role-play a discussion about what to do on the weekend. Use the newspaper ads, or use ads from your local newspaper.

ON-THE-STREET INTERVIEWS

running time — 1:04

Do you know what time it is?

 View Read each exercise and then watch the video for the answers.

A Complete the questions and answers, according to what they say in the video.

1.
> Do you know what time it is?

> _____.

Lorayn

2.
> Could you tell me what time it is?

> Sure. Um, it is _____.

Vanessa

3.
> Excuse me. Do you have the time?

> Oh, sure. _____.

Stephan

4.
> Could you tell me what time it is?

> It is _____ minutes _____.

Blanche

5.
> And _____ the movie?

> It is _____.

Alexandra

6.

By the way, _____ _____ now?

Um . . . _____.

7.

Do you know what the date is?

I believe it's the _____ of _____.

Angelique

 B Choose the correct answer for each question.

1. Where is Vanessa?
   a. In the park.
   b. At the theater.
   c. On the street.

2. Where are Blanche and Herb?
   a. In the park.
   b. At the theater.
   c. At a basketball game.

3. Where is Alexandra?
   a. In the park.
   b. On the street.
   c. At a concert.

4. What time is *National Treasure*?
   a. At 5:00.
   b. At 6:00.
   c. At 5:30.

Extend These exercises will help improve your fluency.

 C Answer the questions. If possible, use the prepositions of time and place in your answers.

1. What time is it? _____

2. What is the date today? _____

3. When is your birthday? _____

4. When is your English class? _____

5. Where is your class? _____

6. Where is your house or apartment? _____

7. Where are you now? _____

 Speaking option: **Ask your partner the same questions.**

UNIT 6
Do you like this blouse?

Social Language
- Express likes
- Describe clothes

Vocabulary
- Clothes
- Colors and other descriptive adjectives
- Verbs *want, have, need, like*

Grammar
- *This / that / these / those*
- The simple present tense

Preview These exercises will help prepare you for the language in the video.

Expand your vocabulary

Clothes

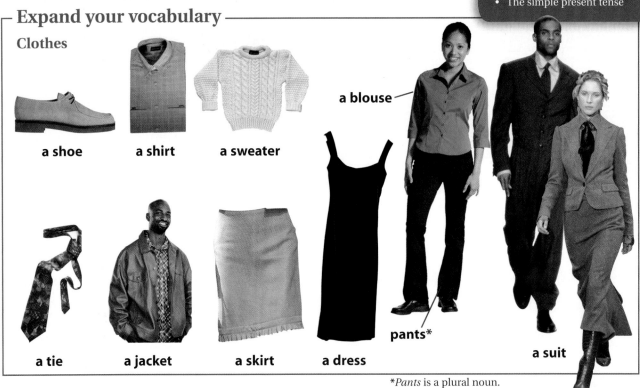

a shoe   a shirt   a sweater

a blouse

a tie   a jacket   a skirt   a dress   pants*   a suit

Pants is a plural noun.

Expand your vocabulary

Colors and other descriptive adjectives

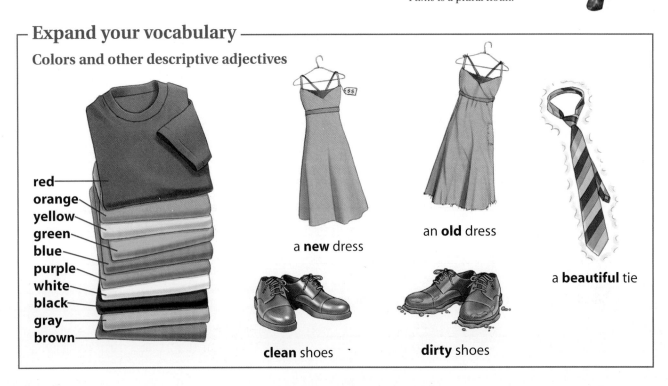

red
orange
yellow
green
blue
purple
white
black
gray
brown

a **new** dress

an **old** dress

a **beautiful** tie

clean shoes

dirty shoes

Describe the clothes.

1. _____a white shirt_____

2. _____

3. _____

4. _____

5. _____

6. _____

Activate your grammar

This, that, these, those

And what about **these** sweaters?

this tie   **that** tie   **these** shoes   **those** shoes

 Complete the descriptions of the clothes. Use *this, that, these,* and *those*.

1. _____This_____ tie is red.
   _____That_____ tie is blue.

2. _____ sweater is green.
   _____ sweater is white.

3. _____ are brown.
   _____ are black.

4. _____ jacket is _____.
   _____ jackets are _____.

5. _____ shirt is _____.
   _____ shirts are _____.

41

I like those sweaters.

Activate your grammar

The simple present tense

Affirmative and negative statements

I
You
We   } **like (don't like)** those shoes.
They
Sara and Jim

He
She   } **likes (doesn't like)** those shoes.
Paula

Questions

Do {you / they} **like** red shoes?   Yes, {I / we / they} **do**.   No, {I / we / they} **don't**.

Does {he / she} **like** the shirt?   Yes, {he / she} **does**.   No, {he / she} **doesn't**.

Contractions
do not → **don't**
does not → **doesn't**

C Complete each statement with the simple present tense of the verb *like*.

1. Ellen _____ red clothes. She _____ blue or green. And she definitely
   _____(not)_____
   _____(not)_____ like anything black.

2. I _____ gray suits, but my husband _____ gray suits. He _____ blue suits.
                                                        (not)

3. My sisters _____ black dresses. But they _____ black shoes. They _____
                                                              (not)
   other colors, such as red or brown for shoes.

D Complete each question with the verb *like*.

1. A: _____ those shoes?
   B: No, I don't.

2. A: _____ your parents _____ that
      old T-shirt?
   B: No. They absolutely don't. They only
      like new ones.

3. A: _____ your sister _____
      white blouses?
   B: Yes, actually, she does.

4. A: _____ ties?
   B: No, he doesn't.

Sneak peek

You look like a movie star— Julia Roberts!

View Read each exercise and then watch the video for the answers.

A Check ☑ the clothes that Cheryl shows Paul and Bob.

☐ 1. a black suit
☐ 2. a purple blouse
☐ 3. blue pants
☐ 4. brown shoes
☐ 5. a blue and white dress

☐ 6. an old jacket
☐ 7. a new tie
☐ 8. a red sweater
☐ 9. a gray sweater
☐ 10. an orange skirt

Language in use

I **really** like those shoes.

I like those shoes. (+)
I **really** like those shoes. (+++)

B Complete the scripts, according to what they say in the video.

_____ this _____?

_____.

_____ blouse is _____.

1.

What about _____?
_____ them?

I _____.

I really _____
_____.

2.

And what about _____?

I really _____
_____ dress!

You _____?

3.

And _____?

_____ is very _____.

4.

43

Expand your vocabulary

Verbs *want*, *have*, and *need*

She **wants** those shoes.

He **needs** a tie.

She **has** a sweater.

Activate your grammar

The simple present tense: information questions

Who has blue shirts?	Robert does.
What do you need?	A new suit.
Which skirt do you like?	The brown skirt.
When do they want the sweaters?	On Monday.

 Circle the correct words to complete each conversation.

1. **A:** (What / Which / When) do you (want / have) for your birthday?
   B: I want a new suit.

2. **A:** (Which / Who / When) shoes does Tom (likes / like)?
   B: He (likes / like) the brown shoes.

3. **A:** Who (want / wants) this sweater?
   B: Fran (do / does).

4. **A:** (Where does / Where do / When do) they (have / has) nice coats?
   B: At the mall.

5. **A:** (Who needs / What needs / Who need) a new suit?
   B: Rob (do / does). He (needs / need) a new suit for a party.

6. **A:** (When does / What does / Which does) she need a blue jacket?
   B: On Wednesday.

 On a separate sheet of paper, write a video script in which two friends talk about the clothes they have, want, need, and like. One friend invites the other to go shopping.

A: I need new shoes.
B: Great! Let's go shopping.

 Speaking option: Act out your video script with a partner.

ON-THE-STREET INTERVIEWS

Do you like that color?

running time — 1:05

View Read each exercise and then watch the video for the answers.

A Complete the interviewer's sentences, according to what he says in the video.

1.

That's a _____ _____.

Why, thank you.

San

2.

That's a _____ color _____.

Thank you very much.

Dan

3.
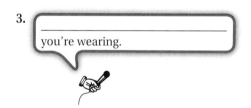

_____ you're wearing.

Thank you. I like it, too.

Martin

4.

_____ often wear _____?

Not always.

Lorayn

5.
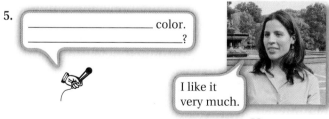

_____ color. _____?

I like it very much.

Vanessa

B ▷ Correct each of the following false statements.

doesn't need

1. Martin ~~needs~~ new shoes.

5. Vanessa's blouse is red.

2. Vanessa's blouse is old.

6. San's sweater is yellow.

3. Dan doesn't like blue.

7. Two people need new shoes.

4. Lorayn really doesn't like red.

Extend   These exercises will help improve your fluency.

C ▷ Answer the questions about yourself.

1. Do you need new clothes or shoes?

_____

4. What color clothes do you like?

_____

2. Do you have new clothes or shoes?

_____

5. When do you wear a suit?

_____

3. What color shoes do you like?

_____

6. Who in your family likes new clothes?

_____

Speaking option: Ask your classmates the same questions.

D ▷ Make a list of all the clothes you see in the video. Then circle the clothes you like.

a green and yellow tie	

E ▷ Write about the people and the clothes you see in the video.

San needs new shoes.
I like Vanessa's blouse.

Speaking option: With a partner, discuss the people and the clothes you see in the video.

UNIT 7
Welcome to my new apartment.

Social Language
• Describe a home

Vocabulary
• Houses and apartments
• Rooms
• Furniture and appliances

Grammar
• *There is / there are,*
  How many, and *a lot of*
• Prepositions of place

Preview These exercises will help prepare you for the language in the video.

Expand your vocabulary

Houses and apartments

a stairway

an apartment

the third floor

an office

an elevator

the second floor

a balcony

the first floor

a lobby

a window

a garden   a door   a garage

a house   **an apartment building**   **an office building**

Expand your vocabulary

Rooms

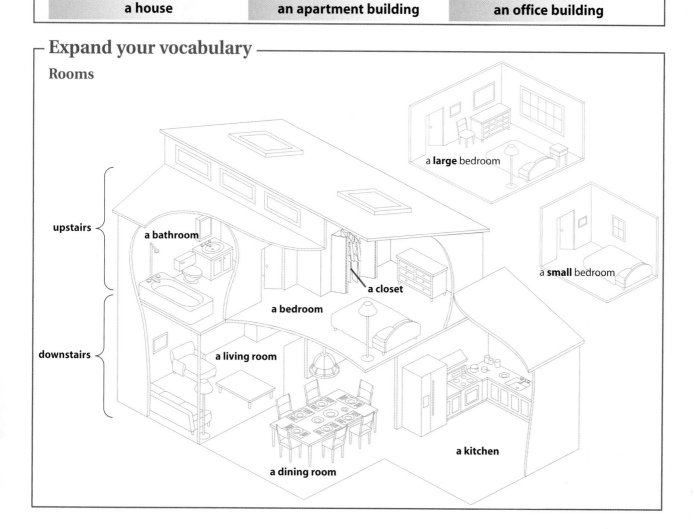

a **large** bedroom

upstairs

a bathroom

a **small** bedroom

a closet

a bedroom

downstairs

a living room

a kitchen

a dining room

47

Write the names of the rooms.

1. _____
2. _____
3. _____
4. _____
5. _____
6. _____

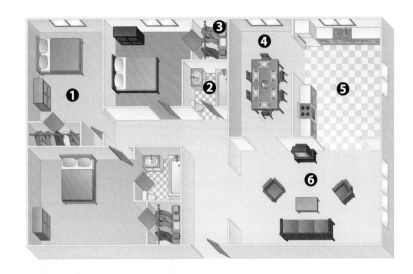

Expand your vocabulary

Furniture and appliances

a sofa

an easy chair

a TV

a picture

a rug

a bed

a lamp

a dresser

a desk

a table

a freezer

a chair

a stove

a microwave

a dishwasher

a refrigerator

a mirror

a bathtub

a sink

a shower

a toilet

Name furniture and other things in each room.

1. Name five things in the bedroom.
    <u>a bed,</u>
    _____

2. Name four things in the living room.
    _____

    _____

3. Name four things in the kitchen.
    _____

    _____

4. Name two things in the dining room.
    _____

    _____

5. Name five things in the bathroom.
    _____

    _____

Write the names of the furniture and appliances you have in your own home.

in my living room	in my bedroom	in my kitchen	in my bathroom

SITCOM

running time — 2:24

View Read each exercise and then watch the video for the answers.

Sneak peek

But where's the bedroom?

A Check ☑ the names of the rooms you hear in the video.

- ☐ 1. the kitchen
- ☐ 2. the bathroom
- ☐ 3. the bedroom
- ☐ 4. the living room
- ☐ 5. the dining room

B Complete the scripts, according to what they say in the video.

The view here is _____ too, Mom.

The _____ is just _____. And my _____ is _____.

1.

It's a little small, but _____. There's the _____, the _____, and the _____.

2.

Why's the _____ in the _____?

_____ no place else for it to go.

3.

I'm afraid to ask about the _____!

4.

50 UNIT 7

C Correct each of the following false statements about Cheryl's apartment.

Welcome to my apartment, Mom!

doesn't live
1. Cheryl ~~lives~~ at 24 Oak Street.

2. Cheryl doesn't like the view from her apartment.

3. The park is just around the corner.

4. Cheryl's office is across the street.

5. Cheryl's mother says the refrigerator is old.

6. Cheryl's mother says the kitchen is very large.

7. Cheryl's mother doesn't like the sofa and the chairs.

Extend These exercises will help improve your fluency.

There are no other rooms.

Activate your grammar

There is / there are, How many, and *a lot of*

Use *there is* with singular nouns. Use *there are* with plural nouns.
There's one **bedroom** in my apartment.
There are large **windows** in their kitchen.

Yes / no **questions and answers**
Are there a lot of stairways in that building?   Yes, there are. / No, there aren't.
Is there a large lobby?   Yes, there is. / No, there isn't.

Ask questions about quantity with *How many*.
How many doors **are there** in your garage?

Use *a lot of* and a plural noun to talk about a large number.
There are **a lot of windows** on the first floor.

D Answer the questions about your own house or apartment.

1. Are there a lot of houses or apartment buildings on your street?
   _____

2. How many bedrooms are there in your house or apartment?
   _____

3. Is there a big kitchen?
   _____

4. Is there a balcony?
   _____

5. Are there a lot of windows?
   _____

6. How many bathrooms are there?
   _____

7. How many closets do you have?
   _____

Language in use
But where are the other rooms, honey?

honey (informal) = name for children, husbands, and wives, etc.

Write about Cheryl's apartment, according to what they say and what you see in the video. Use *There is* and *There are*.

Cheryl has a new apartment. There are . . .

 Speaking option: With a classmate, describe Cheryl's apartment.

Activate your grammar

Prepositions of place

in
She lives **in** an apartment.
I work **in** an office.

at
I live **at** 34 Bank Street.
He works **at** home.

on
He lives **on** Circle Street.
They live **on** the third floor.

across from

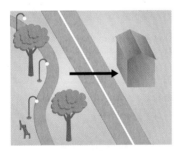

The house is **across from** the park.

around the corner from

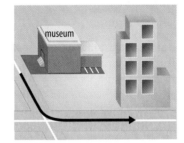

The office is **around the corner from** the museum.

between

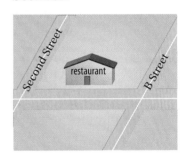

The restaurant is **between** Second Street and B Street.

 Write about where you live and the places in your neighborhood. Use the prepositions of place.

I live at 50 Center Street, across from the train station. There is a restaurant . . .

Some places
a pharmacy
a post office
a travel agency
a bank
a newsstand
a convenience store
a bookstore

ON-THE-STREET INTERVIEWS

Do you live in a house or an apartment?

running time — 1:11

View

Read each exercise and then watch the video for the answers.

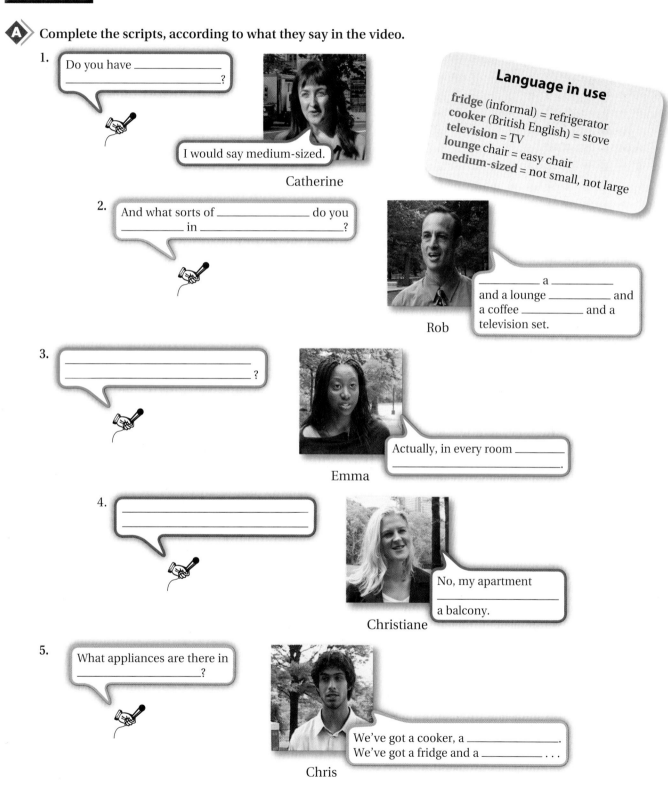

A Complete the scripts, according to what they say in the video.

1.
> Do you have _____
> _____?

I would say medium-sized.

Catherine

Language in use

fridge (informal) = refrigerator
cooker (British English) = stove
television = TV
lounge chair = easy chair
medium-sized = not small, not large

2.
> And what sorts of _____ do you
> _____ in _____?

_____ a _____
and a lounge _____ and
a coffee _____ and a
television set.

Rob

3.
> _____
> _____?

Actually, in every room _____
_____.

Emma

4.
> _____
> _____

No, my apartment
_____
a balcony.

Christiane

5.
> What appliances are there in
> _____?

We've got a cooker, a _____.
We've got a fridge and a _____ . . .

Chris

53

B Complete each statement with the correct person.

| Catherine | Emma | Chris | Christiane |

1. _____ has a medium-sized living room.

2. _____ has an apartment with a lot of windows.

3. _____ doesn't have a balcony in her apartment.

4. _____ lives in a house.

5. _____ likes the colors of her apartment.

6. _____ has a lot of appliances in the kitchen.

 C Correct each of the following false statements.

1. Rob lives in a house.

2. Chris lives in an apartment.

3. Christiane says she has a medium-sized living room.

4. Rob has two sofas in his living room.

5. Emma lives in a house.

6. Emma doesn't have a lot of windows.

7. Christiane's apartment has a balcony.

Extend These exercises will help improve your fluency.

D Write questions to ask about a house or apartment you want. Ask about the number of rooms, the furniture and appliances, the location, and so on.

> How many rooms are there?
> Is there a park nearby?

Speaking option: **Compare your house or apartment with that of a classmate.**

UNIT 8
What do you do in the morning?

Preview These exercises will help prepare you for the language in the video.

Social Language
- Describe daily activities

Vocabulary
- Daily activities at home
- Household chores and leisure activities
- Time expressions

Grammar
- The simple present tense: third-person singular spelling rules
- The simple present tense: habitual activities
- Frequency adverbs
- Questions with *How often*

Expand your vocabulary

Some daily activities at home

| **get up** | **get dressed** | **shave** | **put on my makeup** | **take a shower / take a bath** |

MEALS
breakfast
lunch
dinner

eat breakfast   **make dinner**   **go to bed**

Expand your vocabulary

Some leisure activities

watch TV

sleep late

exercise

take a nap   **read**   **check my e-mail**

55

Activate your grammar

The simple present tense: third-person singular spelling rules

To form the third-person singular:
Add *-s* to most verbs.

| gets | makes | shaves | combs | plays |

Add *-es* to verbs that end in *-s, -sh, -ch,* or *-x.*

| relaxes | brushes | watches |

But remember:

| do → **does** | go → **goes** | have → **has** | study → **studies** |

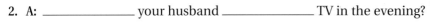

I **get** up at 9:00.
He **gets** up at 8:00.

We **watch** TV in the morning.
She **watches** TV at night.

A Complete the conversations.

before 8:00 **at** 8:00 **after** 8:00

1. **A:** Do you get up early?
   B: No, I _____, but my wife _____.
   She _____ before 6:00, but I _____ after 9:00.

2. **A:** _____ your husband _____ TV in the evening?
   B: No, he _____, but I _____. I _____ TV after dinner.

3. **A:** What time _____ you _____ to bed?
   B: I _____ at 11:00. My wife _____ at 10:00.

4. **A:** When _____ you _____ your e-mail?
   B: I _____ in the evening after I _____ dinner.

5. **A:** Does your brother make dinner in the evening?
   B: No, he _____. I _____ in the evening, and he _____
   breakfast in the morning.

6. **A:** Do you sleep late on the weekend?
   B: No, _____, but my husband _____. Sometimes I _____
   a nap in the afternoon.

Expand your vocabulary

Household chores

wash the dishes

do the laundry

go shopping

clean the house

take out the garbage

Activate your grammar

The simple present tense: habitual activities

Use the simple present tense for habitual activities.

	M	T	W	T	F	S	S
I wash the dishes **every day**. → | ✓ | ✓ | ✓ | ✓ | ✓ | ✓ | ✓ |

We clean the house **on Saturdays**.

	M	T	W	T	F	S	S
						✓	
						✓	

She does the laundry **once a week**.
He goes shopping **twice a week**.
They exercise **three times a week**.

	M	T	W	T	F	S	S
		✓					
		✓	✓				
		✓	✓		✓		

B Complete each sentence with the simple present tense and a time expression.

1.
M	T	W	T	F	S	S
				✓		
				✓		
My sister / go shopping

My sister goes shopping on Fridays.

4.
M	T	W	T	F	S	S
✓						
✓						
I / do the laundry

2.
M	T	W	T	F	S	S
	✓		✓			
We / clean the house

5.
M	T	W	T	F	S	S
✓		✓		✓		✓
My wife and I / exercise

3.
M	T	W	T	F	S	S
✓	✓	✓	✓	✓	✓	✓
The students / check e-mail

6.
M	T	W	T	F	S	S
✓	✓	✓	✓	✓	✓	✓
She / take a shower

Activate your grammar

Frequency adverbs

100% ↑ always — I **always do** the laundry on the weekend.
usually — I **usually exercise** early in the morning.
sometimes — I **sometimes go** to work late.
0% never — I **never go** shopping on weekdays.

You never sleep late?

C Complete each statement, using *always, usually, sometimes,* or *never.* (✓ = does, ✗ = doesn't)

1. Marian ___always___ goes shopping on Saturdays.

2. Charlie _____ goes to concerts.

3. Linda _____ takes the bus to work.

4. Peter _____ walks in the park on weekends.

5. Victoria _____ sleeps late.

6. Lester _____ reads on the train to work.

7. Vivian _____ goes to the movies on Friday nights.

8. Brian _____ watches TV after dinner in the evening.

SITCOM
running time — 1:43

View Read each exercise and then watch the video for the answers.

A Complete each statement with the correct time.

1. Paul always gets up after _____.

2. Marie usually gets up at _____.

3. On weekends, Marie usually gets up at _____.

B Check ☑ the activities Marie says she does in the morning.

☐ make breakfast   ☐ go to bed   ☐ take a nap   ☐ wash the dishes
☐ watch TV   ☐ read the newspaper ☐ exercise   ☐ get dressed
☐ take out the garbage ☐ go shopping   ☐ clean the house   ☐ put on her makeup
☐ do the laundry   ☐ check her e-mail   ☐ take a shower   ☐ go to work

C Choose the best word or phrase to complete each statement.

1. Marie says she _____ after she gets up in the morning.
   a. makes breakfast, takes out the garbage, and does the laundry
   b. makes breakfast, cleans the house, and goes shopping
   c. eats breakfast, takes out the garbage, and washes the dishes

2. Marie says she _____ takes a nap in the morning.
   a. always
   b. sometimes
   c. never

3. Marie says she exercises on _____.
   a. Monday, Wednesday, and Friday
   b. Monday, Tuesday, and Wednesday
   c. Monday, Wednesday, and Saturday

4. Marie says she _____ before she goes to work.
   a. takes a shower, washes the dishes, and cleans the house
   b. takes a shower, gets dressed, and puts on her makeup
   c. takes a bath, gets dressed, and cleans the house

5. Paul says he does the laundry _____.
   a. in the evening
   b. on Monday and Friday
   c. in March and September

Language in use

Wow. You never sleep late?

Wow = !!!

Extend These exercises will help improve your fluency.

D Write a short paragraph about Marie. Describe her daily activities.

On weekdays, Marie usually . . .

Expand your vocabulary

More daily and leisure activities

brush my teeth   **comb / brush my hair**   **come home**   **get undressed**

listen to music   **play soccer**   **hang out with friends**

E Write about your typical day.

On weekdays, I usually . . .

 Speaking option: Tell a classmate about your typical day.

Activate your grammar

Questions with *How often*

How often do you brush your teeth?	Twice a day.
How often does he watch TV?	Every evening.

 Write a question with *How often* for each answer.

1. _How often does Paul go shopping?_ _____

   Paul goes shopping every Saturday.

2. _____

   Carla goes to concerts twice a month.

3. _____

   Louis sleeps late every weekend.

4. _____

   Pat and Bill run in the park three times a week.

5. _____

   Victor walks to work once a week.

6. _____

   Frank plays soccer twice a month.

7. _____

   Bob and Beth do the laundry every evening.

What about you? Answer the questions in your *own* words.

1. How often do you do the laundry?

   _____

2. How often do you exercise?

   _____

3. When do you usually get up in the morning?

   _____

4. What do you usually do in the morning?

   _____

5. Do you sometimes sleep late?

   _____

Speaking option: Ask a classmate the same questions. Then tell your class about your classmate.

ON-THE-STREET INTERVIEWS

What do you usually do during the week?

running time — 1:10

View   Read each exercise and then watch the video for the answers.

A   Complete the statement about each person. Write the letter on the line.

1. Angelique ____.

2. Jessica ____.

3. Deepti ____.

4. Alvino ____.

5. Blanche ____.

6. Lisa ____.

a. never takes naps in the afternoon
b. usually eats breakfast before 7:00 A.M.
c. usually eats lunch at noon

d. usually eats dinner before 7:00 P.M.
e. goes to the movies on weekdays
f. usually sleeps late

B   Complete each statement with the name of the correct person.

Alvino Jessica Deepti Angelique

1. _____ likes an early dinner.

2. _____ eats an early breakfast.

3. _____ goes to the movies on weekdays.

4. _____ is pretty busy in the afternoon.

C   Complete the scripts, according to what they say in the video.

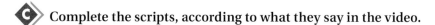

1. _____ during the week, um . . . I mean,
I _____ to a couple of films. I _____
to _____ to the movies . . .

(continued on page 62)

2. I don't _____ in the
   afternoon. I don't get a chance to.

3. I love to _____ around 6:00,
   which is not too _____, because if
   it's too _____, I can't sleep.

Extend
These exercises will help improve your fluency.

D Write something about each person.

1. Angelique: _She usually . . ._ _____
   _____

2. Jessica: _____
   _____

3. Deepti: _____
   _____

4. Alvino: _____
   _____

5. Blanche: _____
   _____

6. Lisa: _____
   _____

Speaking option: Choose a person from the interviews and tell a partner about him or her.

E Are you a morning person or an evening person? Explain your answer. Describe the things you usually do in the morning or in the evening.

> _I'm an evening person because I usually sleep late and I usually go to bed late. I like evening because . . ._

A **morning person** gets up early
and goes to bed early.
An **evening person** gets up late
and goes to bed late.

Speaking option: Tell a partner why you are a morning person or an evening person.

TOP NOTCH POP SONG On the Weekend

running time — 2:09

A Listen to the song "On the Weekend." Then listen again without looking at the screen and complete the lyrics with verbs in the simple present tense.

On the weekend, when we _____, there is always so much joy and laughter.
1.
On the weekend, we never think about the days that _____ before and after.
2.

He _____ every morning. Without warning, the bedside clock rings the alarm.
3.
So he _____— he does his best to be on time.
4.
He _____ his hair, goes down the stairs, and _____ some breakfast.
5.   6.
A bite to eat, and he feels fine.

Yes, he's on his way to one more working day.

On the weekend, when we _____, there is always so much joy and laughter.
7.
On the weekend, we never think about the days that _____ before and after.
8.

On Thursday night, when he _____ from work,
9.
he _____, and if his room's a mess, he _____ the house.
10.   11.
Sometimes he takes a rest.

Maybe he _____ something delicious, and when he's done
12.
he _____ all the pots and dishes, then _____.
13.   14.
He knows the weekend's just ahead.

On the weekend, when we _____, there is always so much joy and laughter.
15.
On the weekend, we never think about the days that _____ before and after.
16.

B Listen to the song again. Write three things he does after he gets up every morning.

1. He _____.

2. He _____.

3. He _____.

C Write at least four things he does (or sometimes does) when he comes home on Thursday night before going to bed.

1. He _____.

2. He _____.

3. He _____.

4. He _____.

What are you doing this weekend?

Social Language
• Make plans to get together

Vocabulary
• Time expressions

Grammar
• The present continuous for actions in progress and future plans

Preview These exercises will help prepare you for the language in the video.

Activate your grammar

The present continuous

Use the present continuous for actions in progress and for future plans.
Use a form of *be* and a present participle.

I'**m watching** TV. [action in progress]
I'**m going** to class tomorrow. [future plan]

Look at the spelling patterns for the present participle.

talk → **talking**	mak~~e~~ → **making**
read → **reading**	tak~~e~~ → **taking**
watch → **watching**	com~~e~~ → **coming**

But remember:

shop → shopping   get → getting

Yes / no questions

Are you **reading** right now?	Yes, I am.	No, I'm not.
Is she **watching** TV?	Yes, she is.	No, she's not. / No, she isn't.
Are they **shopping**?	Yes, they are.	No, they're not. / No, they aren't.

Information questions

Who's driving?	Sarah is.
What are you **doing?**	Studying.
Where are they **going?**	To the park.

> I'm taking an art class from 1:00 to 3:00.

Expand your vocabulary

Time expressions

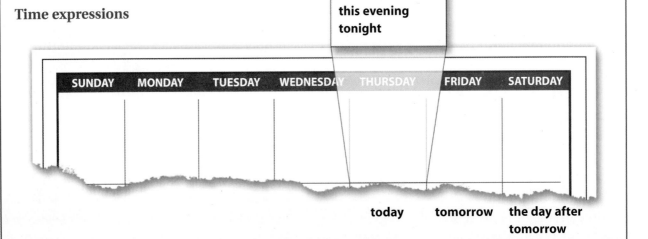

THURSDAY
this morning
this afternoon
this evening
tonight

SUNDAY	MONDAY	TUESDAY	WEDNESDAY	THURSDAY	FRIDAY	SATURDAY

today   tomorrow   the day after tomorrow

A Choose the best word or phrase to complete each statement.

1. Tomorrow I _____ to work.
   a. am going   **b.** going   **c.** is going

2. They _____ right now.
   a. studying   **b.** study   **c.** are studying

3. What _____ tomorrow morning?
   a. you doing   **b.** are you doing   **c.** do you do

4. Mr. and Mrs. Black _____ in the kitchen.
   a. are eating   **b.** eating   **c.** they eating

5. Who _____ to the movies with you?
   a. go   **b.** going   **c.** is going

6. When _____ TV?
   a. she is watching   **b.** is she watching   **c.** she watches

7. _____ to the early show?
   a. We going   **b.** Are we going   **c.** We go.

B Complete each statement with a form of the present continuous.

1. They _____ plans for this afternoon.

make

2. What _____ you _____ on Tuesday?

do

3. When _____ she _____ lunch tomorrow?

eat

4. Who _____ on the phone right now?

talk

5. Where _____ we _____ tonight?

meet

SITCOM

running time — 1:55

What are you doing this weekend?

View Read each exercise and then watch the video for the answers.

A Complete the scripts, according to what they say in the video.

1. **Marie:** How about Saturday _____?

   Cheryl: _____ breakfast for some friends at 9:00.

2. **Cheryl:** How about 3:30?

   Marie: No. _____ with a friend from 3:00 to 4:00. Then _____ to the movies at 5:00 with _____.

3. **Cheryl:** Sunday _____?

   Marie: _____ my _____ until _____.

4. **Marie:** Sunday _____?

   Cheryl: _____ to a baseball _____ with _____ at 1:00.

Choose the correct answer for each question.

1. Why can't Cheryl go shopping on Saturday morning?
   a. Because she's making breakfast for some friends.
   b. Because she's doing the laundry.
   c. Both of the above.

2. What's Cheryl doing on Saturday afternoon?
   a. She's taking a class.
   b. She's doing the laundry.
   c. She's exercising with a friend.

3. Who's Marie going to the movies with?
   a. Her parents.
   b. Her sister.
   c. Some friends.

4. What's Marie doing on Sunday morning?
   a. Going to a baseball game.
   b. Visiting her parents.
   c. Making breakfast.

5. Who's going to the baseball game with Cheryl?
   a. Bob.
   b. Paul.
   c. Cheryl's mother.

6. What are Paul and Bob going to do the next day?
   a. Play baseball.
   b. Go shopping.
   c. Play basketball.

 Rewrite each of the following false statements to make them correct.

1. On ~~Sunday~~ morning, Cheryl's making ~~lunch~~ for some friends.
   On Saturday morning, Cheryl's making breakfast for some friends.

2. Marie's doing laundry on Saturday afternoon.
   _____

3. Cheryl's taking a cooking class at 3:00 on Saturday.
   _____

4. Cheryl's meeting a friend at the art museum on Saturday morning.
   _____

5. Cheryl's going to a baseball game with Marie on Saturday afternoon.
   _____

6. Cheryl and Marie are going to the movies on Saturday afternoon at around 1:00.
   _____

Extend   These exercises will help improve your fluency.

D Fill out the date book with <u>your</u> plans for this week.

Monday
English class 3:00–6:00 P.M.

Tuesday
Meet Tim at the museum 2:30 P.M.
Call Mom 9:00 P.M.

Wednesday
Go shopping with sis 5:00 P.M.

_____ Monday

_____ Tuesday

_____ Wednesday

_____ Thursday

_____ Friday

_____ Saturday

_____ Sunday

E Write one statement for each day you have plans. Use the present continuous.

> On Monday, I'm eating at the World Café with my friend Jamie.

 Speaking option: Tell a classmate about your plans for this week.

F On a separate sheet of paper, write a video script for a conversation between two friends who want to get together. Use your own date book for information.

> What are you doing this weekend? Do you want to go shopping with me?

> That sounds great.

 Speaking option: Act out your script with a classmate.

ON-THE-STREET INTERVIEWS

running time — 1:04

What are you doing this evening?

 View Read each exercise and then watch the video for the answers.

A Complete the scripts, according to what they say in the video.

1.
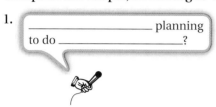
_____ planning to do _____?

_____ I'm planning to go to dinner _____ and maybe some drinks.

Joe

2.
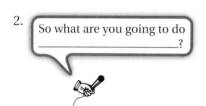
So what are you going to do _____?

I'm going to go to _____ and maybe see _____ and _____.

San

3.

That's interesting. And will you be going with anyone?

With _____ in the _____ and her _____.

Martin

4.
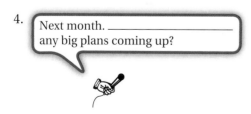
Next month. _____ any big plans coming up?

Um, _____ major plans coming up _____.

Stephan

B Choose the best answer for each question.

1. What's Martin doing this evening?
   a. Going to the opera.
   b. Staying home and having dinner.
   c. Going to the movies with friends.

2. Where's San going to be next Monday?
   a. At work.
   b. In the park.
   c. At the movies.

3. Who's Joe having dinner and drinks with?
   a. Martin.
   b. Some friends.
   c. His family.

4. Who's going to the opera?
   a. Martin.
   b. San.
   c. Joe.

5. What's San doing after work next Monday?
   a. Having dinner.
   b. Watching TV.
   c. Both.

Extend These exercises will help improve your fluency.

C Write one sentence about each person's plans. Use the present continuous whenever possible.

1. (Joe, this evening) _Joe's having dinner with friends this evening._

2. (Martin, this evening) _____

3. (Martin, this weekend) _____

4. (San, this weekend) _____

5. (San, next Monday) _____

D Write five interview questions about future plans. Use the present continuous.

1. _What are you doing tonight?_ _____

2. _____

3. _____

4. _____

5. _____

E Answer the questions in Exercise D with information about yourself.

1. _____

2. _____

3. _____

4. _____

5. _____

Speaking option: Ask a classmate your questions and write the answers.

UNIT 10
Tonight, I'm cooking.

Preview These exercises will help prepare you for the language in the video.

Social Language
• Discuss ingredients for a recipe

Vocabulary
• Drinks and foods: count and non-count nouns
• Places to keep food in a kitchen
• Containers and quantities
• Verbs for preparing food

Grammar
• Count and non-count nouns
• *How many* and *Are there any*
• *How much* and *Is there any*
• The simple present tense and the present continuous

Expand your vocabulary

Foods: count nouns

Vegetables

an onion

a tomato

a potato

beans

a pepper

peas

carrots

a tomato → tomato**es**
a potato → potato**es**

Fruits

a lemon

an apple

an orange

a banana

Activate your grammar

Count nouns

Count nouns can be singular or plural.
  I want **an orange**.   I like **peas**.   There are **three onions**.

How many and *Are there any*

Use *How many* and *Are there any* with plural count nouns.
  How many potatoes **are there** on the shelf?   There are three.
  How many lemons **are there** on the counter?   There aren't any.
  Are there any bananas on the counter?   Yes, there are.
  Are there any onions in the fridge?   No, there aren't [any].

in the fridge

on the shelf

on the counter

Look at the photos on page 71 again. Complete each question with *How many* or *Are there any*. Fill in all the blanks. Then answer each question.

1. A: *Are there any* _____ tomatoes on the counter?

   B: *Yes, there are* _____ .

2. A: _____ oranges _____ in the fridge?

   B: _____ .

3. A: _____ apples in the fridge?

   B: _____ .

4. A: _____ onions _____ on the shelf?

   B: _____ .

5. A: _____ lemons on the shelf?

   B: _____ .

6. A: _____ potatoes _____ on the counter?

   B: _____ .

7. A: _____ peppers _____ in the fridge?

   B: _____ .

Expand your vocabulary

Drinks and foods: non-count nouns

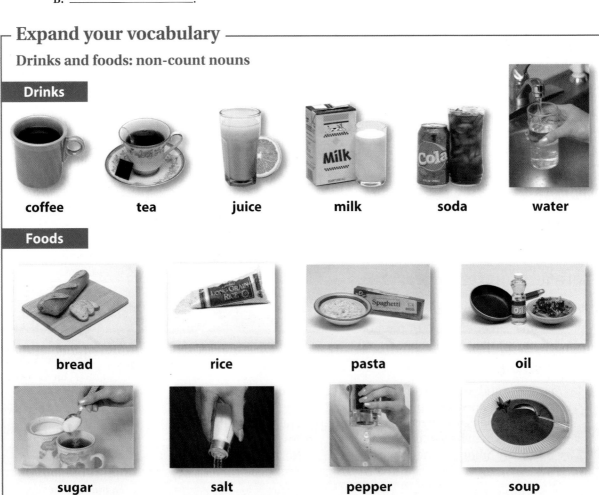

Drinks

coffee   tea   juice   milk   soda   water

Foods

bread   rice   pasta   oil

sugar   salt   pepper   soup

 Complete each statement with a container or quantity.

1. There's _____ soda in the fridge.

2. There's _____ potatoes on the shelf.

3. Is there _____ tea on the counter?

4. There's _____ oil on the shelf.

5. There's _____ bread on the table.

Activate your grammar

Bananas are fruit.

Non-count nouns

Non-count nouns are not singular or plural.
  I like **pasta**. (NOT ~~a pasta~~ and NOT ~~pastas~~)

BE CAREFUL! Always use singular verbs with non-count nouns.
  There**'s** juice in the fridge. (NOT ~~There are~~ juice in the fridge.)

How much and *Is there any*

Use *How much* and *Is there any* with non-count nouns.
  How much juice **is there** in the fridge? There are two bottles.
  How much rice **is there** on the counter? There's one bag.
  Is there any bread on the shelf? Yes, there is.
  Is there any sugar on the table? No, there isn't [any].

BE CAREFUL! Use *How many* and *Are there any* with plural count nouns.
  How many lemons are there in the fridge?
  (NOT ~~How much~~ lemons . . . ?)
  Are there any oranges on the shelf?
  (NOT ~~Is there any~~ oranges . . . ?)

> **Some nouns can be either count or non-count.**
>
> I like *cabbage*.   There's *a cabbage* in the fridge.
>
> There isn't any *soda*.   I want *a soda*.

 Circle the correct words. Write the noun. Write count nouns in the plural form.

1. (How many)/ How much) _____ (are there / is there) in the fridge?
   <u>onion</u>

2. (How many / How much) _____ (are there / is there)?
   <u>tea</u>

3. (Are there any / Is there any) _____ on the shelf?
   <u>coffee</u>

4. (How many / How much) _____ (are there / is there)?
   <u>potato</u>

5. (Are there any / Is there any) _____ on the counter?
   <u>bean</u>

6. (How many / How much) _____ (are there / is there) in the fridge?
   <u>juice</u>

7. (How many / How much) _____ (are there / is there)?
   <u>salt</u>

8. (Are there any / Is there any) _____ on the table?
   <u>bread</u>

Sneak peek

Tonight, I'm cooking.

 View Read each exercise and then watch the video for the answers.

A What does Bob want for his soup? Check ☑ the foods.

☑ onions	☐ bread	☑ cabbage	☑ bananas	☐ carrots
☐ an apple	☐ rice	☑ a potato	☐ salt	☑ a lemon
☑ tomatoes 2	☑ peas	☐ peppers	☑ sugar	☑ coffee
☑ beans	☐ an orange	☐ juice	☐ pepper	☐ tea

B Correct each of the following false statements.

       Bob   *Cheryl*

1. ~~Cheryl~~ is making soup for ~~Bob~~ and Marie.

2. Marie has fruits and vegetables in her fridge.

3. There are ~~three~~ *2* tomatoes in the fridge.

4. Cheryl ~~doesn't have~~ *has* any sugar.

                               one

5. Bob wants ~~two~~ lemons.

                 are two

6. ~~There's a can~~ of soup on the counter.

7. Marie and Cheryl ~~don't~~ like Bob's soup.

8. Marie ~~doesn't~~ like*s* the bananas and coffee in Bob's soup.

C Complete the scripts, according to what they say in the video.

Do you have any vegetables?

1.

I have some *onions*, *tomatoes* . . .

How many tomatoes?

2. I have some *bean*, some *peas*, one *cabbage*, and *a potato*.

You put *bananas* in your vegetable *soup*?

2.

Sounds good, doesn't it? Now *do you have* any *sugar*?

And I ___need a lemon___. Oh, and do you have any ___coffee___?

Do you have a recipe for this?

___Go watch TV___, please.

3.

Extend

These exercises will help improve your fluency.

Expand your vocabulary

More count and non-count foods and drinks

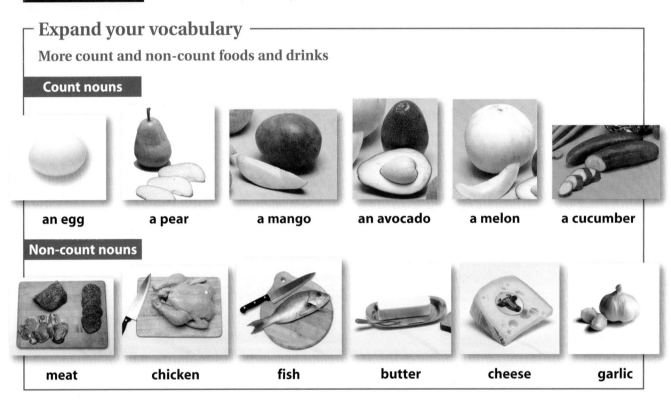

Count nouns

an egg   a pear   a mango   an avocado   a melon   a cucumber

Non-count nouns

meat   chicken   fish   butter   cheese   garlic

What foods and drinks do you like? Use plural count nouns or non-count nouns.

Fruits:	
Vegetables:	
Drinks:	

Speaking option: Ask your classmates about the foods and drinks they like.

Do you like tea?

No, I don't. I like coffee.

Expand your vocabulary

Verbs for preparing food

 Boil a large pot of water.

 Slice the cabbage.

 Cook the pasta.

 Sprinkle the cabbage with salt.

 Drain the pasta.

 Put the cabbage in the fridge.

 Chop the garlic.

 Melt the butter.

 Sauté the garlic in oil.

 Add pepper.

 Mix the garlic and pasta.

E Describe a recipe. Use the vocabulary.

Name of recipe: _____

Ingredients: _____

_____

_____

_____

1. _____

2. _____

3. _____

_____

_____

_____

_____

Recipe: Fruit Salad

Ingredients:
apples
bananas
oranges
lemon juice
sugar

1. Slice the apples and bananas.
2. Chop the oranges.
3. Add lemon juice and sprinkle with sugar.
4. Mix the ingredients.

Speaking option: **Tell a classmate about your recipe.**

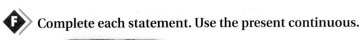

What **are** you **making?**

Activate your grammar

The simple present tense and the present continuous

Use the present continuous for actions that continue in the present.
    She**'s draining** the pasta.   They**'re chopping** the onions.

Use the simple present tense for habitual actions
    We never **boil** milk.   I always **put** sugar in my coffee.
    (NOT We ~~are never boiling~~ milk.)   (NOT I ~~am always putting~~ sugar in my coffee.)

Use the simple present tense with *want, need,* and *like.*
    We **need** butter.   (NOT We ~~are needing~~ butter.)

And I **need** a lemon.

F Complete each statement. Use the present continuous.

1. Bob _____ soup.
           make

2. Bob _____ the soup.
           mix

3. Marie _____ the vegetables on the counter.
   put

4. Bob _____ a can of soup.
   open

G Complete each question with a verb from the box. Then answer the questions with true information about yourself. Use *always, usually, sometimes,* or *never.*

put	cook	eat	sprinkle	drink

> Do you put bananas in the fridge?
> I never put bananas in the fridge.

1. Do you _____ sugar in your tea or coffee?

   (YOU) _____

2. Do you _____ eggs for breakfast?

   (YOU) _____

3. Do you _____ dinner?

   (YOU) _____

4. Do you _____ salt on your food?

   (YOU) _____

5. Do you _____ water with your meals?

   (YOU) _____

Speaking option: Ask a classmate the questions. Then tell your class about your classmate.

ON-THE-STREET INTERVIEWS

What do you like to eat and drink?

running time — 1:10

 View Read each exercise and then watch the video for the answers.

A Write the letters of the foods and drinks each person likes.

1.  ___f__ C D B
   Ian

a.

b.

2.  D B
   James

c.

d.

3.  A E
   Dan

e.

f.

B Circle the correct words to complete each statement.

1. Natalie (usually eats / doesn't usually eat) carrots.

2. James (usually eats / doesn't usually eat) a lot of soup.

3. Dan (sometimes eats / never eats) soup.

4. Matt (usually eats / doesn't usually eat) soup.

Language in use

I have soup **occasionally.**

occasionally = sometimes

C Check ☑ all the correct answers.

1. James has _____ in his fridge right now.

   ☑ vegetables   ☐ fruits   ☐ meat   ☐ tea   ☐ butter

2. Ian has _____ in his fridge right now.

   ☐ vegetables   ☑ cheese   ☑ eggs   ☑ bread   ☐ milk   ☐ butter

3. Dan is eating lunch at about _____ today.

   ☐ 12:30   ☐ 1:30   ☑ 3:00   ☐ 3:30

4. Lorayn wants sushi for _____.

   ☐ breakfast   ☐ lunch   ☑ dinner

Extend   This exercise will help improve your fluency.

D Answer the questions.

1. What do you eat every day for breakfast?	**6. How often do you eat soup?**
2. How about for lunch?	**7. How often do you drink coffee or tea?**
3. And what about for dinner?	**8. What do you have in your fridge right now?**
4. How often do you eat vegetables?	**9. What are you having for lunch tomorrow?**
5. How often do you eat salad?	**10. What do you want for dinner tomorrow?**

Speaking option: Ask a classmate the questions. Tell your class about your classmate.

UNIT 11
How was your trip?

Social Language
• Discuss a trip

Vocabulary
• Past-time expressions
• Leisure-time activities
• Weather expressions
• Seasons

Grammar
• The past tense of *be*
• The simple past tense

Preview These exercises will help prepare you for the language in the video.

Expand your vocabulary

Past-time expressions

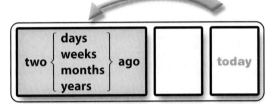

Activate your grammar

The past tense of *be*

Affirmative and negative statements

I
He **was** at home last night.
She

We
You **were** classmates at school.
They

It **wasn't** an exciting game.

They **weren't** on the bus.

Questions and answers

Was she there last year?   Yes, she was. / No, she wasn't.
Where were they last month?   They were in Europe.
When was she in France?   She was there two years ago.

But, Dr. Anderson, you **were** in London and you **didn't see** the city.

Contractions
was not → **wasn't**
were not → **weren't**

Activate your grammar

The simple past tense

Add *-ed* to form the simple past tense. If the verb ends in *-e*, just add *-d*.
call → call**ed**   like → lik**ed**
I **called** my mother two days ago, but she wasn't home.

To make negative statements, use *didn't* (*did not*) and the base form of a verb.
I **didn't go** on a trip last year. (NOT I didn't ~~went~~ on a trip last year.)

I
you
Did he   I
she **watch** TV last night?   Yes, you **did**.
we   he
they   she
                                 No, we **didn't**.
                                      they

What **did** you **do** yesterday?   **Where / when / how did** she go?
Who went there with Marie?   **Who did** they **see**?

Irregular verbs			
come	→ **came**	meet	→ **met**
do	→ **did**	put	→ **put**
drive	→ **drove**	read	→ **read**
eat	→ **ate**	ride	→ **rode**
get	→ **got**	see	→ **saw**
give	→ **gave**	sit	→ **sat**
go	→ **went**	take	→ **took**
have	→ **had**	wake	→ **woke**
leave	→ **left**	wear	→ **wore**
make	→ **made**	write	→ **wrote**

A **Change each sentence from the present to the past.**

1. We ~~are~~ *were* in Italy.

2. Who wants the newspaper?

3. When do you take vacation?

4. Where is the movie?

5. How do you get there?

6. They aren't late; they're early.

7. We like that restaurant.

8. Does the house have three bedrooms? Yes, it does.

9. Who has brown shoes?

10. It's a great movie. I love it.

B **Answer each question with a complete sentence and real information.**

1. When was your last vacation?

   My last vacation was two years ago.

   _____

2. Where did you go?

   _____

3. Did you have a good time?

   _____

4. What did you see there?

   _____

5. Who went with you?

   _____

C **Write statements using each of the following past-time expressions.**

1. (yesterday)

   _____

2. (last week)

   _____

3. (last month)

   _____

4. (two months ago)

   _____

5. (last year)

   _____

SITCOM

running time — 1:55

Sneak peek

Well, hello, Dr. Anderson! Welcome back.

Thank you very much.

View Read each exercise and then watch the video for the answers.

A Mark each statement *T* (true) or *F* (false).

____ 1. Dr. Anderson just came back from London.

____ 2. She went to London for vacation.

____ 3. She went shopping in London.

____ 4. She went to the movies in London.

____ 5. She gave two speeches.

____ 6. She didn't see the city because she loved the hotel.

____ 7. Marie thought Dr. Anderson had a bad vacation.

____ 8. Dr. Anderson said London looked nice from her hotel.

London

B Complete the scripts, according to what they say in the video.

Marie: _____ your trip to London?
          1.

Dr. Anderson: _____ fine, thank you.
               2.

Marie: _____ you _____ lots of museums?
        3.   4.

Dr. Anderson: No. I _____ any.
                    5.

Marie: _____ you _____ in some good restaurants?
        6.   7.

Dr. Anderson: No. I _____ in the same bad restaurant every day.
                    8.

Marie: _____ you _____ any plays or concerts?
        9.   10.

Dr. Anderson: No. But I _____ TV in the hotel room at night.
                        11.

Marie: _____ you _____ some nice walks around London?
        12.   13.

Dr. Anderson: Actually, no. I _____ in a chair for four days.
                              14.

C Write four or more statements about what Dr. Anderson did when she was in London, according to the video.

She met doctors from all over the world.

D Write four or more statements about what Dr. Anderson *didn't do* when she was in London, according to the video.

She didn't visit any museums.

Extend These exercises will help improve your fluency.

Expand your vocabulary

Leisure-time activities

1. go to the beach

2. go running

3. go bike riding

4. go swimming

5. go for a drive

6. go for a walk

E Write a statement about each picture. Use the simple past tense and a past-time expression.

1. *They went to the beach last weekend.*

2. _____

3. _____

4. _____

5. _____

6. _____

Expand your vocabulary

Weather expressions

It's cloudy. It's sunny.

It's hot. It's cold.

It's windy.

It's raining. It's snowing. It's warm. It's cool.

F Make notes about a great weekend you had. Use past-time expressions and verbs in the simple past tense.

When	Where	With whom	Weather	Activities
two weeks ago	at the beach	school friends	sunny and warm	swam, went for walks

When	Weather
Where	
	Activities
With whom	

G On a separate sheet of paper, write a short description of your weekend.

Speaking option: Tell a classmate about your weekend.

ON-THE-STREET INTERVIEWS

What did you do last weekend?

running time — 1:10

 View Read each exercise and then watch the video for the answers.

A Write the verbs in the simple past tense.

a. (go) _____ to a movie

b. (work) _____ outside

c. (read) _____ the paper

d. (relax) _____

e. (have) _____ dinner with a friend

f. (go) _____ to the public library

g. (go) _____ running

h. (have) _____ drinks with friends

Now watch the video and write the letters of the activities next to the people who did them. Some people did more than one activity.

1.   2.   3.   4.

Rob: ___ ___ ___ ___   Maiko: ___ ___   Mauro: ___   Alvino: ___

B Complete the questions and responses, according to what they say in the video.

1.

_____ last weekend?

I _____.

Last weekend, I _____ _____ in the _____.

2.

This past _____, _____ the weather like?

It was _____, _____, pleasant.

It was . . . oh, last _____ it _____ too good. Uh, _____ rainy, but I think _____ pretty good. _____.

87

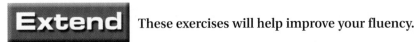

Extend These exercises will help improve your fluency.

Expand your vocabulary

Seasons

| spring | summer | fall / autumn | winter |

C Answer the questions about the weather and the seasons.

1. What's the weather like today? _____

2. Is it hot, cold, warm, or cool today? _____

3. Yesterday, was it sunny, cloudy, or windy? _____

4. What was the weather like last night? _____

5. What's the weather like in the summer? _____

6. What's the weather like in the winter? _____

7. What about the spring and the fall? _____

D Answer the questions about yourself.

1. What did you do last weekend?

_____

2. What was the weather like?

_____

3. Did you have a good time?

_____

Speaking option: Ask a classmate the same questions and discuss what you did.

TOP NOTCH POP SONG My Favorite Day

running time — 3:35

A Listen to the song "My Favorite Day." Mark each statement *T* (true) or *F* (false). Listen again to check your work.

_____ 1. They walked together.

_____ 2. They didn't talk.

_____ 3. They saw the ocean across the beach.

_____ 4. Today is her favorite day of the week.

_____ 5. She wrote this song in the morning.

_____ 6. They said good-bye to each other.

_____ 7. She feels very sad.

B Listen again without looking at the screen and complete the lyrics with the past tense verbs.

Last night we _____ together. It seems so long ago.
1.
And we just _____ and _____. Where _____ the time _____?
2.   3.   4.
We _____ the moonlit ocean across the sandy beach.
5.
The waves of summer fell, barely out of reach.

Yes, that _____ then, and this is now,
6.
and all I do is think about yesterday, my favorite day of the week.

When I _____ this morning, my feelings _____ so strong.
7.   8.
I put my pen to paper, and I _____ this song.
9.
I'm glad I _____ to know you. You really _____ me smile.
10.   11.
My heart belonged to you for a little while.

Yes, that _____ then, and this is now,
12.
and all I do is think about yesterday, my favorite day of the week.

It _____ wonderful to be with you. We _____ so much to say.
13.   14.
It _____ awful when we waved good-bye. Why did it end that way?
15.

Yes, that was then, and this is now,

and all I do is think about yesterday, my favorite day of the week.

UNIT 12
She has a fever.

Social Language
- Talk about ailments
- Describe people

Vocabulary
- Ailments
- Adjectives to describe hair
- Parts of the body
- The face
- Accidents and injuries
- Remedies

Grammar
- Adjectives with *be* and *have*
- *Should* for advice

Preview These exercises will help prepare you for the language in the video.

Expand your vocabulary

Ailments

He has **a headache**.

She has **a stomachache**.

He has **an earache**.

He has **a backache**.

She has **a toothache**.

She has **a cold**.

He has **a sore throat**.

He has **a fever**.

He has **a cough**.

She has **a runny nose**.

I feel { awful. terrible. bad.
I don't feel well.

A Check ☑ ailments you have had or someone you know has had in the past. Write a sentence with a time expression about the person who had the ailment.

	Me	Someone I know	
a headache	☑	☐	*I had a headache last night.*

	Me	Someone I know	
a headache	☐	☐	_____
a stomachache	☐	☐	_____
an earache	☐	☐	_____
a backache	☐	☐	_____
a toothache	☐	☐	_____
a cold	☐	☐	_____
a sore throat	☐	☐	_____
a fever	☐	☐	_____
a cough	☐	☐	_____
a runny nose	☐	☐	_____

Expand your vocabulary

Adjectives to describe hair

black   **brown**   **red**   **blonde**   **gray**   **white**

dark   **light**

straight   **wavy**   **curly**   **short**   **long**

Circle the correct words to complete each statement.

1. Her hair is (short / long) and (straight / wavy).

2. His hair is (dark / light) and (curly / straight).

3. Her hair is (short / long) and (red / blonde).

4. His hair is (curly / wavy) and (gray / black).

5. Write about yourself: My hair is _____ and _____.

Activate your grammar

Adjectives with *be* and *have*

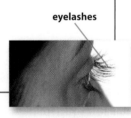
eyelashes

With *be*		With *have*
My eyes **are** blue.	OR:	I **have** blue eyes.
Our hair **is** blonde.	OR:	We **have** blonde hair.
Her eyelashes **are** long and dark.	OR:	She **has** long dark eyelashes.

 Rewrite each statement, using *be*.

1. He has short, wavy hair.
   His hair is short and wavy.

2. She has brown eyes.
   _____

3. He has long, dark hair.
   _____

4. She has long, blonde eyelashes.
   _____

5. She has curly, red hair.
   _____

6. He has green eyes.
   _____

7. She has wavy, white hair.
   _____

8. He has long, straight hair.
   _____

Read each exercise and then watch the video for the answers.

Sneak peek

Oh, no! I forgot! Tell him I don't feel well and I'm going to the doctor.

A Check ☑ the ailments Paul says Marie has.

☐ 1.　☐ 2.　☐ 3.　☐ 4.　☐ 5.

☐ 6.　☐ 7.　☐ 8.　☐ 9.　☐ 10.

B Mark each statement *T* (true) or *F* (false).

_____ 1. Marie doesn't feel well.

_____ 2. Marie is having lunch with her mother.

_____ 3. Marie is going to the doctor.

_____ 4. Marie has a sore throat.

_____ 5. Mr. Evans is calling the doctor.

C Complete the scripts, according to what they say in the video.

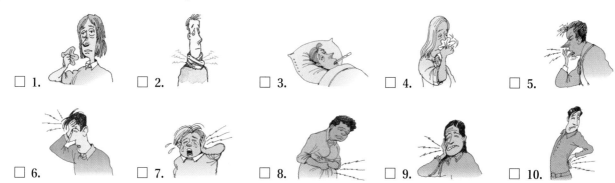

I'_____ for lunch.

Aren't you _____ with Mr. Evans?

1.

_____?

Uh, no. She's not feeling so well.

She _____.

2.

3.

She _____. And _____. And _____. And _____.

That sounds _____.

_____ jacket.

You do look _____!

I do?

4.

Extend These exercises will help improve your fluency.

Expand your vocabulary

Parts of the body

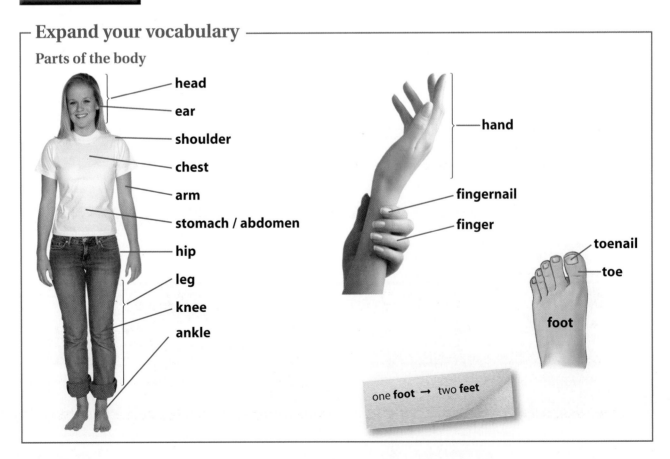

- head
- ear
- shoulder
- chest
- arm
- stomach / abdomen
- hip
- leg
- knee
- ankle

- hand
- fingernail
- finger

- toenail
- toe
- foot

one **foot** → two **feet**

Expand your vocabulary

Accidents and injuries

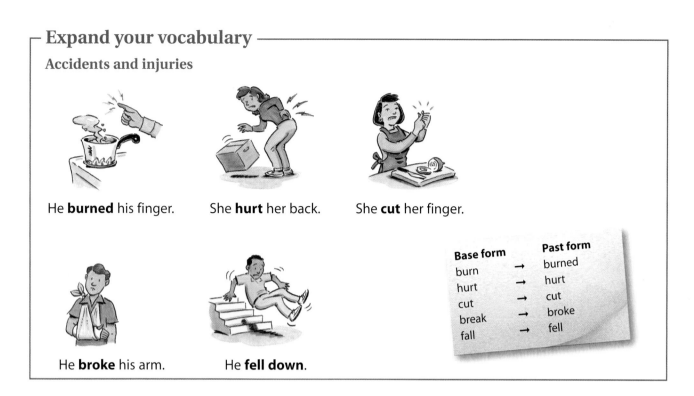

He **burned** his finger.　　She **hurt** her back.　　She **cut** her finger.

He **broke** his arm.　　He **fell down**.

Base form		Past form
burn	→	burned
hurt	→	hurt
cut	→	cut
break	→	broke
fall	→	fell

D Describe accidents or injuries you have had or someone you know has had.

> Two weeks ago, I hurt my foot in a soccer game.

Speaking option: Tell your classmates about the accidents and injuries you wrote about.

Expand your vocabulary

Remedies

take something　　**lie down**　　**have some tea**　　**see a doctor / dentist**

Activate your grammar

Should for advice

Ask for and give advice with *should* or *shouldn't* and the base form of a verb.

Questions
- **Should** I **see** a doctor?
- **Should** she **take** something?
- What **should** she do?

Answers
- Yes, you **should**.
- No, she **shouldn't**.
- She **should go** to bed.

He has a fever.

He **shouldn't go** to school tomorrow.

I have a bad headache.

You **should take** something.

E Suggest a remedy. Use *should* or *shouldn't* and the base form of a verb.

1. "I have a toothache."

   YOU _____

2. "I feel awful. I think I have a fever."

   YOU _____

3. "Ow! I hurt my back!"

   YOU _____

4. "My sister has a runny nose and a sore throat."

   YOU _____

5. "I have a terrible cold, but I'm going to work today."

   YOU _____

6. "My father has an earache. He feels terrible."

   YOU _____

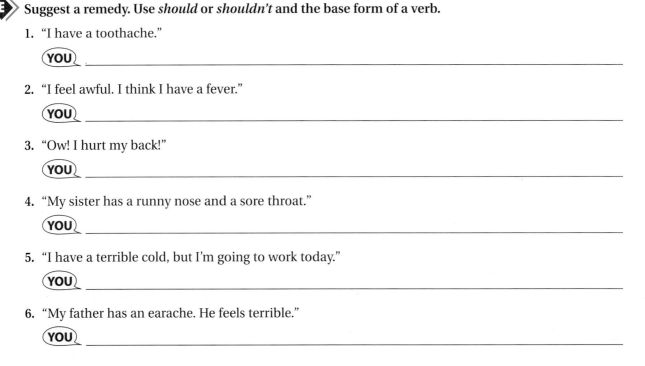

Speaking option: Role-play a conversation with a classmate. You don't feel well or you had an accident. Your classmate gives advice or suggests remedies.

What do your parents look like?

View Read each exercise and then watch the video for the answers.

A Choose the correct word or phrase to complete each statement.

Jessica describes her _____.
a. mother
b. father
c. mother and father
d. sisters and brothers

1.

Martin describes his _____.
a. mother
b. father
c. mother and father
d. brothers and sisters

2.

> **Language in use**
> my **dad** (informal) = my father
> my **mom** (informal) = my mother
> a handsome **guy** (informal) = a handsome man
> a **sibling** = a brother or sister

Angelique describes her _____.
a. sister
b. brother
c. father
d. mother

3.

B Complete each statement.

1. Jessica's _____ is very handsome. _____ has big _____ and _____ hair.

2. Jessica's _____ is beautiful. _____ has _____ black hair and big _____ eyes.

3. Martin's _____ have _____ hair and _____ eyes, just like him.

4. Martin says his _____ are very pretty.

5. Angelique says her _____ is very handsome.

Complete the questions and responses, according to what they say in the video.

1.
> Could you describe _____
> _____ for me?

> My dad is like this _____.

2.
> Could you tell me what one of
> _____ looks like?

> Um, looks _____ a little bit.

> Could you describe them a little bit—
> their _____, their _____?

> Uh, they both have _____ hair
> and _____ eyes, just like me.

3.
> And how about _____?
> Are they _____?

> I'd say they're _____.

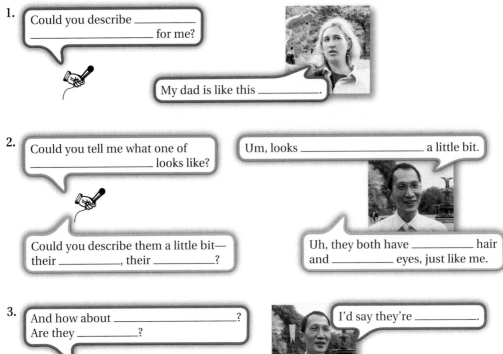

Extend These exercises will help improve your fluency.

Expand your vocabulary

The face

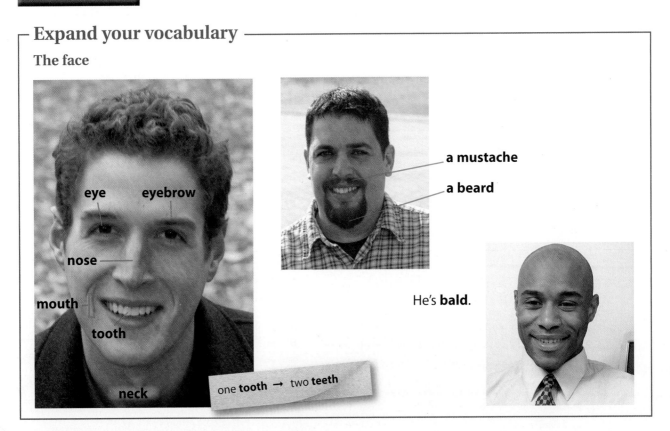

eye   eyebrow

nose

mouth

tooth

neck

a mustache

a beard

He's **bald**.

one **tooth** → two **teeth**

D Describe some of the people in your family.

Name: Jody   Relationship: sister
Description: My sister Jody is very pretty. She has long eyelashes and short
                curly hair.

Name: Relationship:
Description:

Name: Relationship:
Description:

Describing people

pretty   short
handsome   young
good-looking   old
beautiful   big
cute   small
tall

Describing hair

black   white   wavy
brown   dark   curly
red   light   short
blonde straight long
gray

Describing eyes

brown
blue
green

Name: Relationship:
Description:

Speaking option: Tell your classmates about some of the people in your family.

UNIT 13
Could you do me a favor?

Social Language
• Request favors

Vocabulary
• Abilities and skills

Grammar
• Requests with *Could* or *Can*
• *Can* and *can't* for ability

Preview These exercises will help prepare you for the language in the video.

Activate your grammar

Requests with *Could* or *Can*

Use questions with *Could you* or *Can you* and the base form of a verb to make requests. *Could you* and *Can you* have the same meaning. Use *please* to make a request more polite.

**Could you please
open the window?**
(OR: Can you please)

**Could you please
close the door?**
(OR: Can you please)

**Could you please
turn on the light?**
(OR: Can you please)

**Could you please
turn off the TV?**
(OR: Can you please)

**Could you please
help me?**
(OR: Can you please)

**Could you please
hand me my glasses?**
(OR: Can you please)

A ▷ Complete the requests, using *Could you* or *Can you* and the base form of a verb.
(Remember: *Could you* and *Can you* have the same meaning.)

1. ___Could you___ please ___pass___ the sugar? I can't reach it.

2. _____ please _____ the garbage? I'm pretty busy right now.

3. _____ please _____ home a little early today? I have to go out to a meeting and the kids are home.

4. I'm going to bed. _____ please _____ the lamp?

5. It's cold in here. _____ please _____ the window?

SITCOM

running time — 1:37

 View   Read each exercise and then watch the video for the answers.

A   Mr. Evans asks Marie to do some things for him. Put them in order.

_____ buy a cup of coffee

_____ fix his car

_____ play the violin

_1_ buy a tie

_____ get a newspaper

_____ buy a shirt

_____ buy a suit

play the violin

fix a car

B   Choose the best word or phrase to complete each statement.

1. Mr. Evans needs a new tie because _____.
   a. his tie is dirty
   b. his client needs a tie
   c. he doesn't like his tie

2. Mr. Evans asks Marie to get a _____ at the store on the corner.
   a. tie
   b. newspaper
   c. cup of coffee

3. Mr. Evans wants more coffee because _____.
   a. his coffee is cold
   b. he spilled his coffee
   c. a new client is coming in an hour

4. Mr. Evans says he needs a new shirt because _____.
   a. his shirt doesn't look nice
   b. he spilled coffee on his shirt
   c. he doesn't like the color

5. Mr. Evans also asks Marie to get him a _____.
   a. violin
   b. suit
   c. car

6. Mr. Evans says he's going to the store to buy a _____.
   a. shirt
   b. suit
   c. tie

Language in use

Certainly.

Certainly (very formal) = OK.

C Complete Mr. Evans's requests. Then complete Marie's responses with words and phrases from the box.

Mr. Evans: _____ go to the store and buy _____
1.
for me?

Marie: _____ .
3.

Mr. Evans: And _____ get a _____ for me at the store on
4.   5.
the corner?

Marie: _____ .
6.

Mr. Evans: This _____ is _____ . _____ buy me
7.   8.   9.
a cup of _____ , too?
10.

Marie: _____ .
11.

Mr. Evans: Also, this _____ doesn't look very _____ .
12.   13.
_____ buy me a new _____ ?
14.   15.

Marie: _____ .
16.

Mr. Evans: _____ get me a _____ , too?
17.   18.

Marie: _____ .
19.

Mr. Evans: And _____ play the violin for me _____ ?
20.   21.

Marie: _____ .
22.

Mr. Evans: _____ tonight?
23.

Marie: _____ .
24.

Box:
Certainly	Yes, sir
Yup	Yes
Sure	Of course
Sure, no problem	

Speech bubble: I'm having lunch with a client in an hour, and I spilled coffee on my tie.

D Look at Mr. Evans's requests again. Check ☑ the ones you think he *really* wants Marie to do.

☐ buy coffee for him   ☐ buy a tie   ☐ buy a shirt   ☐ fix his car
☐ get a newspaper   ☐ buy a suit   ☐ play the violin

Extend These exercises will help improve your fluency.

E Write a request for one person in each of the following situations. Write a response to each request.

1. a wife and a husband at home
   A: (request) _____
   B: (response) _____

2. two people eating at the same table
   A: (request) _____
   B: (response) _____

3. two colleagues at work
   A: (request) _____
   B: (response) _____

Speaking option: Act out your requests and responses with a partner.

Activate your grammar

Can and *can't*

To talk about ability, use *can* or *can't* and the base form of a verb.

Questions
Can you **play** the guitar?
Can he **speak** English?

Short answers
Yes, I **can**. / No, I **can't**.
Yes, he **can**. / No, he **can't**.

can not = **cannot** = **can't**

She **can play** the guitar.   He **can't cook**.

Expand your vocabulary

Abilities and skills

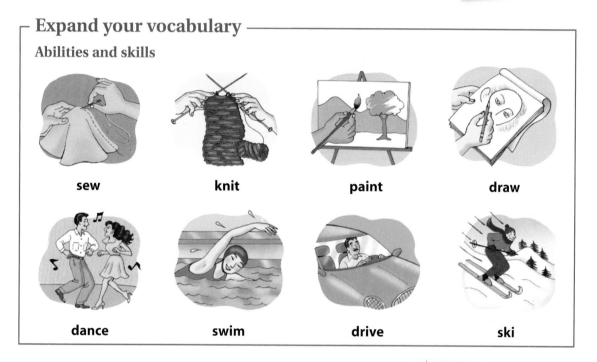

sew   knit   paint   draw

dance   swim   drive   ski

 Write statements about your abilities or the abilities of your friends or family members. Use *can* and *can't*.

I can fix a car, but my brother can't.

1. _____

2. _____

3. _____

4. _____

5. _____

ON-THE-STREET INTERVIEWS

Can you play a musical instrument?

running time — 1:40

View Read each exercise and then watch the video for the answers.

A Complete each statement with the correct name.

Stephan   Matt   Elli   San   Vanessa

1. _____ says she can sing.

2. _____ says he learned to play the guitar when he was young.

3. _____ says he played the drums when he was young.

4. _____ says she runs every day.

5. _____ says she can dance.

6. _____ says he can speak Greek and Italian.

7. _____ says she can cook and ride a bike.

B Complete the scripts, according to what they say in the video.

1.
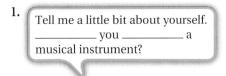
Tell me a little bit about yourself. _____ you _____ a musical instrument?

Not at all. I wish I _____, but I _____.

I _____ a musical instrument. Um, but I like to _____, so that's kind of related to music.

2.
Do you speak any foreign languages?

_____. I speak, uh, _____ foreign languages.

3.
Can you _____ or _____ or _____ or cook?

Yes to a lot of those things. I _____ a little bit. Um, I _____ ride _____.

 These exercises will help improve your fluency.

C Answer the questions about your skills and abilities. If you don't have the skill, write about someone else who does.

1. Can you play a musical instrument?
   _____

2. Can you swim or ski?
   _____

3. Can you paint or draw?
   _____

4. Can you knit or sew?
   _____

5. Can you drive or fix a car?
   _____

Can you play a musical instrument?
No, I can't, but my father can.

D Write about your skills and abilities. Use *can* and *can't*.

Things you can do	Things you can't do

Speaking option: Discuss your skills and abilities with a classmate. Talk about the skills and abilities of other people in your family.

UNIT 14
I'd like to get married.

Social Language
- Discuss future plans
- Announce good news
- Congratulate someone

Vocabulary
- Life events
- Free-time activities
- Academic subjects

Grammar
- *Would like*
- *Be going to* for the future
- Conditions and results in the future

Preview These exercises will help prepare you for the language in the video.

Expand your vocabulary

Life events

| **be born** | **grow up** | **go to school** | **move** | **study** |

| **graduate** | **get married** | **get divorced** | **have children** |

Activate your grammar

Would like

How many children **would** you **like to have**?   We**'d like to have** two or three.
What **would** she **like to study**?   She**'d like to study** business.
Would she **like to study** medicine?   Yes, she **would**. / No, she **wouldn't**.

business

medicine

I'd like to get married and **have** children.

I would like → **I'd like**

A Complete each sentence about yourself, using *I'd like to* or *I wouldn't like to*.

1. _____ get married this year.

2. _____ have six children.

3. _____ paint my bedroom next month.

4. _____ buy a new car this year.

5. _____ write a book.

6. _____ learn another language.

7. _____ study medicine.

8. _____ move to a new apartment.

Activate your grammar

Be going to for the future

Next month, my sister **is going to have** a baby.
I'm going to learn French.
They**'re not going to buy** a new car.

Are you **going to study** psychology?   Yes, I am. / No, I'm not.
Who**'s going to graduate** this week?   My brother.
When **are** your friends **going to get** married?   Next week.

We're going to go to a movie tonight.

psychology

B Write statements and questions with *be going to*.

1. I / see a dentist / this morning _____.

2. We / have a baby / in April _____.

3. My brother / graduate / in May _____.

4. Where / they / study psychology _____?

5. Who / make dinner / tonight _____?

6. When / you / go on vacation _____?

Sneak peek

I'm so happy for you!

View Read each exercise and then watch the video for the answers.

A Complete each statement. Write the letter on the line.

1. Marie would like to ____.

2. If she can't live in China, Marie is going to ____.

3. Paul would like to ____.

4. Paul is going to ____.

5. Bob and Cheryl would like to ____.

6. Bob and Cheryl are going to ____ tonight.

a. get married and have children

b. learn to speak Chinese

c. write a book about cooking

d. live in China

e. go to a movie

f. learn to play the guitar

B Mark each statement *T* (true) or *F* (false).

____ 1. Marie would like to know Bob and Cheryl's plans for the future.

____ 2. Marie doesn't think Paul is going to write a book about cooking.

____ 3. Paul says he's going to learn to cook.

____ 4. Bob would like to get married but he wouldn't like to have children.

____ 5. Marie and Paul would like to get married.

____ 6. Paul would like to go to the movies with Bob and Cheryl.

C Complete the scripts, according to what they say in the video.

1. **Marie:** If _____,
   I_____ to speak
   _____.
   Paul: I'm going to _____.
   Marie: Really? About what?
   Paul: _____. Cooking.

2. **Bob:** I'd like to get married and have children, too.
   Marie: Really? _____?
   Paul: You want to _____?!
   Cheryl: Actually, _____ some news
      _____.
   Marie: No! _____?!
   Bob: _____ you to
      _____ with us.
   Marie: Oh.
   Bob: And _____.

Extend These exercises will help improve your fluency.

Expand your vocabulary

Free-time activities

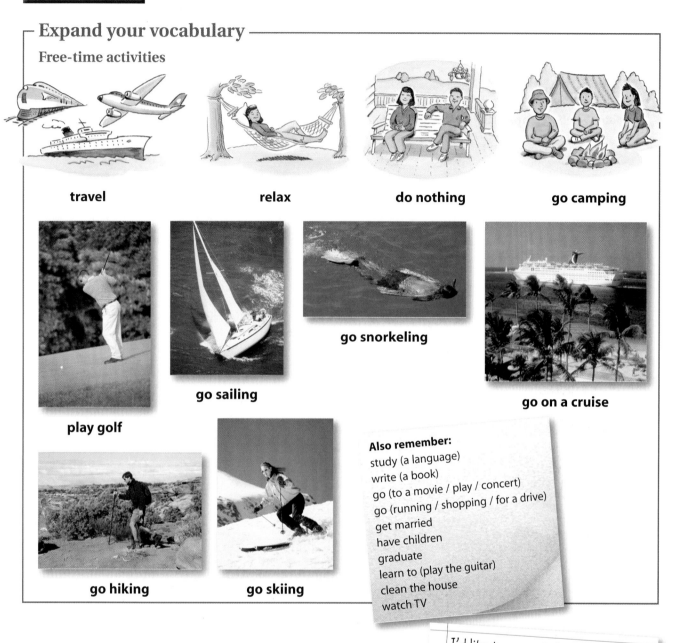

travel   relax   do nothing   go camping

play golf   go sailing   go snorkeling   go on a cruise

go hiking   go skiing

Also remember:
study (a language)
write (a book)
go (to a movie / play / concert)
go (running / shopping / for a drive)
get married
have children
graduate
learn to (play the guitar)
clean the house
watch TV

I'd like to go snorkeling next summer.

D What activities would you like to do? Write sentences with *I'd like to.* Use the vocabulary or other activities you know.

1. (this weekend) _____

2. (next week) _____

3. (next month) _____

4. (next year) _____

5. (next summer) _____

 Speaking option: Tell your classmates what activities you'd like to do.

Where were you born?

View Read each exercise and then watch the video for the answers.

A Match each person with a question. Write the name on the line.

| Dan | Christiane | Joe | Ian | Lorayn | Maiko |

1. Who grew up in New York City? _____

2. Who would like to move to Thailand? _____

3. Who studied psychology? _____

4. Who would like to write? _____

5. Who would like to learn to ski? _____

6. Who would like to play the violin? _____

B Mark each statement *T* (true) or *F* (false).

____ 1. Lorayn was born in Thailand.

____ 2. Lorayn was born on January 28, 1969.

____ 3. Ian is going to get married next month.

____ 4. Christiane likes warm weather.

____ 5. Christiane is going to work in Thailand, and then she is going to work in the United States.

C Complete the questions and answers, according to what they say in the video.

1. **Interviewer:** So _____?

   Answer: I _____ in New York City.

   Interviewer: And _____?

   Answer: January 28, 1969.

   Interviewer: And, uh, _____ in New York?

   Answer: Yes, I did.

2. **Interviewer:** Where and _____ study?

   Answer: I _____ at Rutgers, in, New Jersey, and I _____.

3. **Interviewer:** What _____ future plans?

   Answer: I will _____ in America and then maybe _____ to Thailand.

   Interviewer: Why _____ to Thailand?

   Answer: Because Thailand has beautiful beaches and _____ all the time.

 Answer the questions.

1. Where were you born?

   _____

2. When were you born?

   _____

3. Where did you grow up?

   _____

4. Where did you go to school?

   _____

 Speaking option: Ask a classmate the same questions. Tell your classmate about the events in your life.

Language in use

I really love skiing . . . but I'm **not too good at it.**

not too good at something = doesn't do something well

Expand your vocabulary

Academic subjects

Also remember:
business
medicine
psychology

architecture

education

mathematics / math

science

nursing   **engineering**

law

Activate your grammar

Conditions and results in the future

if- clause [condition]	future result
If I **have** the time,	**I'm going to study** nursing.
If I **get** married,	**I'm going to have** lots of children.

Always use the simple present tense or the present tense of *be* in the *if-* clause.

    If I **have** the time . . .   (NOT If I ~~am going to have~~ the time . . .)

An *if-* clause can come at the beginning of the sentence or at the end.

    If the weather is nice, I'm going to play golf.

    I'm going to play golf **if the weather is nice.**

E Choose the correct verb form to complete the conditional sentences.

1. If I _____ enough money, I'm going to buy a big house.
   (have / 'm going to have)

2. If we have enough time, we _____ camping this summer.
   (go / are going to go)

3. If my friends _____ married, they're going to move to New York.
   (get / are going to get)

4. I'm going to clean the house if they _____ tomorrow.
   (visit / are going to visit)

5. If he _____ medicine, he's going to be pretty busy.
   (studies / is going to study)

F Write about your future plans. What would you like to learn or study? What would you like to do?

> If I have time, I'm going to learn Arabic.

Speaking option: Tell your classmates about your future plans.

TOP NOTCH POP SONG I Wasn't Born Yesterday

running time — 1:52

A ▷ Listen to the song "I Wasn't Born Yesterday." Then listen again without looking at the screen and complete the lyrics.

I _____ to school and _____ the lessons of the human heart.
     1.   2.

I _____ an education in _____ and art.
     3.   4.

It doesn't matter what you say. I know the silly games you play.

I _____ born yesterday.
     5.

I _____ born yesterday.
     6.

Well, pretty soon I _____ with a good degree.
            7.

It took some time to understand the way you treated me,

and it's too great a price to pay. I've had enough, and anyway,

I _____ born yesterday.
     8.

I _____ born yesterday.
     9.

So you think _____ marry you and be your pretty wife?
         10.

Well, that's too bad, I'm sorry, now. _____ and get a life!
            11.

It doesn't matter what you say. I know the silly games you play.

I _____ born yesterday.
     12.

I _____ born yesterday.
     13.

B ▷ Mark each statement *T* (true) or *F* (false), according to the song.

_____ 1. He studied medicine.

_____ 2. She finished college.

_____ 3. He didn't treat her well.

_____ 4. He wanted to marry her.

_____ 5. She wanted to marry him.

Video Scripts

Video scripts

Unit 1

Sitcom

Mr. Evans: Hi! Are you Mr. Rashid?

Mr. Rashid: Yes, I am.

Mr. Evans: It's a pleasure to meet you. I'm James Evans, president of Top Notch Travel.

Marie: Welcome to Top Notch. I'm Marie, the receptionist.

Mr. Rashid: Nice to meet you.

Paul: Hi. I'm Paul. I'm a tour guide.

Mr. Rashid: Glad to meet you.

Cheryl: Hi, I'm Cheryl.

Mr. Rashid: The office manager.

Cheryl: Yes!

Mr. Rashid: A pleasure.

Mr. Evans: Bob? Bob is . . .

Mr. Rashid: A chef.

Mr. Evans: No, Bob is not a chef. Bob is a . . . doctor? No, Bob is not a doctor. Bob is not a singer. He's not an architect. He's not an athlete . . . Bob!

Bob: Hi . . . I'm the mailman.

Mr. Evans: Bob!

Mr. Evans: This is Bob. Bob is . . .

Mr. Rashid: An actor!

On-the-Street Interviews

Interviewer: Hi. How are you today?

Dan: Good. How are you?

Interviewer: I'm well. My name's Doug. What's yours?

Dan: Dan.

Interviewer: Hi, Dan. Nice to meet you.

Dan: Nice to meet you.

Interviewer: Hello.

Christiane: Hello.

Interviewer: My name's Doug. What's your name?

Christiane: My name's Christiane.

Interviewer: Hi, Christiane. It's nice to meet you.

Christiane: Nice to meet you too, Doug.

Interviewer: So tell me, what do you do?

Christiane: I work in a hotel.

Interviewer: Good morning.

Vanessa: Good morning.

Interviewer: My name's Doug.

Vanessa: My name's Vanessa.

Interviewer: Hi, Vanessa.

Vanessa: How are you?

Interviewer: I'm well. Thank you. Tell me, what do you do?

Vanessa: I'm a teacher.

Interviewer: Good afternoon.

Emma: Good afternoon.

Interviewer: My name's Doug.

Emma: My name is Emma.

Interviewer: Hi, Emma.

Emma: Hi. Nice to meet you.

Interviewer: Nice to meet you. What do you do?

Emma: I'm a receptionist.

Interviewer: Oh, that's interesting. Well, take care.

Emma: Bye-bye.

Interviewer: Hi. My name's Doug.

Alvino: Hi, Doug.

Interviewer: What's your name?

Alvino: Alvino.

Interviewer: So, Alvino, what do you do?

Alvino: Retail.

Interviewer: You're a businessman?

Alvino: Yes, I am.

Interviewer: Well, it's nice to meet you.

Alvino: Nice to meet you as well.

Interviewer: Take care. Have a nice day.

Alvino: You as well. Bye-bye.

Interviewer: Bye-bye.

Unit 2

Sitcom

Paul: This is good coffee

Bob: It is good

Paul: Who's that?

Bob: That's your friend David Ducain. He's a writer from France.

Cheryl: That's not David Ducain. That's Arturo Montoya. He's Mr. Evans's neighbor. He's a doctor from Mexico.

Marie: No. That's Jeff Davis. He's an artist.

Bob: No. That's Alan Reese. He's our lawyer.

Cheryl: That's not Alan Reese.

Marie: Oh! It's Clark Thomas from England. He's a musician!

Paul: Excuse me.

Waitress: Yes?

Paul: Who's that?

Waitress: That's . . . Mr. Evans. He's . . . your boss.

Bob: That's not Mr. Evans.

Mr. Evans: Hey, guys!

Paul: Musician!?

On-the-Street Interviews

Interviewer: Hi. I'm Doug.

Natalie: Hi. Natalie. This is my husband Chris.

Interviewer: Hi, Chris. Nice to meet you.

Chris: Nice to meet you.

Interviewer: Where are you from?

Natalie: I'm from Oklahoma.

Chris: I'm from Bristol in England.

Interviewer: Hi. What's your name?

Deepti: My name is Deepti Gupta.

Interviewer: That's an interesting name. Could you spell it for me?

Deepti: Yes. The first name is Deepti, which is D-E-E-P-T-I. The last name is Gupta. That's G-U-P-T-A.

Interviewer: And are you from the United States?

Deepti: No, I'm not.

Interviewer: Where are you from?

Deepti: India.

Interviewer: What's your phone number?

Lisa: My phone number is 239-0560.

Interviewer: And your address?

Matt: 43 Concord Square.

Interviewer: Do you have an e-mail address?

Elli: Yep. It's my name, which is Elli Fordyce—E-L-L-I-F-O-R-D-Y-C-E@msn.com.

Interviewer: What's your cell-phone number?

Ian: My cell-phone number is 555-1312.

Unit 3

Sitcom

Tourist: Excuse me. How do I get to the Red Café?

Mr. Evans: The Red Café? Let's see. Go to the corner and turn left.

Tourist: Left.

Mr. Evans: Go two blocks and turn right.

Tourist: Right.

Mr. Evans: Around the corner is the train station.

Tourist: Take the train.

Mr. Evans: Don't take the train! Go through the station, and across the street to the bookstore. Next to the bookstore is a pharmacy. Next to the pharmacy is the Red Café.

Tourist: Yes!

Mr. Evans: Got it? Let's do it again.

Mr. Evans and tourist: Corner. Left. Two blocks. Right. Around the corner. Don't take the train! Through the station, across the street. Bookstore. Pharmacy. Red Café!

Tourist: Thank you very much.

Mr. Evans: You're very welcome.

On-the-Street Interviews

Interviewer: Tell me, uh, is there a bank near here?

Catherine: Actually, there's . . . there's several. Uh . . . there's one on the corner up here, and, uh, one right behind across the street, and then one diagonal.

Interviewer: Excuse me. Is there a newsstand nearby?

Rob: Yes, there is. There's one right down the street, two blocks, make a right, go one block, and it's right on the right-hand side.

Interviewer: OK, so that was go up the street two blocks . . .

Rob: Yes.

Interviewer: Make a right, one block . . .

Rob: Two blocks.

Interviewer: Two blocks . . .

Rob: And it's right on the right-hand side.

Interviewer: Right on the right-hand side.

Interviewer: Do you know if there's a restaurant nearby?

Joe: Yes, there's a great restaurant in the park. Uh, it's called *Tavern on the Green*.

Interviewer: Is there a taxi stand nearby?

Ian: No, there isn't.

Interviewer: Can you tell me how to get to the train station?

Christine: Uh, would you like to walk or take the subway?

Interviewer: Um, I'll walk.

Christine: Just walk straight down this street for about thirty blocks and you'll run right into it.

Interviewer: That's a long walk.

Christine: It is a long walk, but you like to walk, right?

Unit 4

Sitcom

Marie: Is this your family?

Cheryl: Yes.

Marie: Who's this?

Cheryl: My brother.

Marie: He's so handsome. How old is he?

Cheryl: He's thirty-four.

Marie: Oh!

Cheryl: He's a doctor.

Marie: Oh!!

Cheryl: That's his wife.

Marie: Oh. She's very pretty. Who's this?

Cheryl: That's my mother.

Marie: Your mother? But she's so old.

Cheryl: She's not old. She's fifty-eight.

Marie: OK. Who's this? Is he a doctor, too?

Cheryl: No, he's an architect. That's my sister's husband.

Marie: Who's this?

Cheryl: That's my sister's son. He's a university student.

Marie: He's so cute!

Cheryl: He's so young.

Marie: Who's this short old woman? What?

Cheryl: That is not a short old woman. That's me.

Marie: Oh! Sorry.

On-the-Street Interviews

Interviewer: Who's that in the picture in your left hand?

Rita: I have two girls and a boy.

Interviewer: Could you tell me how old your children are?

Rita: Yes. My oldest boy is forty-one, soon to be forty-two. The second one, who is a girl, is forty. And my baby is thirty-four.

Interviewer: Do you have any children?

Mauro: I have two children—a son and a daughter.

Interviewer: Could you tell me a little about them? What do they do? What are their occupations?

Mauro: Oh, they're both students.

Interviewer: Do you have any siblings?

Chris: Yes. I've got one sister who's twenty-six.

Interviewer: Tell me, do you have any brothers or sisters?

Maiko: Yes, um, I have one younger brother.

Interviewer: Tell me, what does he look like? Is he tall?

Maiko: Um, he is very tall, very skinny, very lean.

Interviewer: So is he handsome?

Maiko: Um, yes, he is.

Unit 5

Sitcom

Cheryl: You're late.

Bob: What time is it?

Cheryl: Two minutes after six.

Bob: I am not late. Two minutes is not late.

Cheryl: Yes, it is. It's two minutes late.

Bob: Oh, look! It's five to six. I'm early.

Cheryl: So for your birthday on Saturday, there's a great French movie at the Avalon.

Bob: There's a baseball game on Saturday night.

Cheryl: Or there's a play at the Arts Center at 8 P.M. *Life is a Dream.*

Bob: The Tigers are playing the Giants. You know, baseball?

Cheryl: Oh, look! There's a Mozart concert on Saturday. Would you like to go?

Bob: What time?

Cheryl: Half past seven.

Bob: The ball game's at 7:00.

Cheryl: Oh, wow! There's a talk by the writer Ellen Lee at the University on . . .

Bob: On Saturday night. Is your birthday on Saturday?

Cheryl: No. It's *your* birthday. Would you like to go to a baseball game for your birthday?

Bob: A baseball game! That sounds great!

On-the-Street Interviews

Interviewer: Do you know what time it is?

Lorayn: Five o'clock.

Interviewer: Could you tell me what time it is?

Vanessa: Sure. Um, it is 10:30.

Interviewer: Excuse me. Do you have the time?

Stephan: Oh, sure. It's 4:15.

Interviewer: Thank you.

Stephan: You're welcome.

Interviewer: Could you tell me what time it is?

Blanche: It is . . .

Herb: I can't.

Blanche: It is ten minutes to twelve.

Interviewer: Great. Thanks so much.

Blanche: You're welcome.

Interviewer: What movie do you want to see?

Alexandra: I want to see *National Treasure.*

Interviewer: And what time is the movie?

Alexandra: It's at six o'clock.

Interviewer: By the way, what time is it now?

Alexandra: Um . . . it is 5:30.

Interviewer: So you're right on time.

Alexandra: I am.

Interviewer: Could you tell me what time it is?

Angelique: I actually don't wear a watch, so I'm not really sure.

Interviewer: Do you know what the date is?

Angelique: I believe it's the 29th of September.

Unit 6

Sitcom

Cheryl: Do you like this blouse?

Bob: Yes.

Paul: That blouse is beautiful!

Cheryl: Thank you! What about these shoes? Do you like them?

Bob: I like those shoes.

Paul: I really like those shoes.

Cheryl: And what about this dress?

Bob: I really like that dress!

Cheryl: You do?

Bob: You look like a movie star—Julia Roberts!

Cheryl: I see. And this skirt?

Bob: That skirt is very nice.

Cheryl: Bob. Bob!

Bob: What?!

Cheryl: What about these sweaters?

Bob: I like those sweaters. Those sweaters are beautiful!

Paul: I really like those sweaters. They're really nice.

Cheryl: Thank you!

On-the-Street Interviews

Interviewer: That's a nice sweater.

San: Why, thank you.

Interviewer: That's a nice color shirt.

Dan: Thank you very much.

Interviewer: That's a really nice tie you're wearing.

Martin: Thank you. I like it too.

Interviewer: Is that a new blouse?

Vanessa: Yes, it is. My sister bought it for me.

Interviewer: Do you like that color?

Dan: I do. Navy blue's my favorite color.

Interviewer: Do you often wear black?

Lorayn: Not always. Red's another favorite color of mine.

Interviewer: Is green a favorite color of yours?

Martin: Yes. I also like yellow too.

Interviewer: What other colors do you like to wear?

San: I like wearing blue. Um, I like wearing purples and white.

Interviewer: I like that color. Do you like that color?

Vanessa: I like it very much.
Interviewer: Do you mind if I ask you a question? Not at all.
Interviewer: Do you need new shoes?
Lorayn: I always need new shoes.
San: I always need new shoes.
Natalie: Yes. A woman always needs new shoes.
Interviewer: Tell me, do you need a new pair of shoes?
Martin: I don't think so.

Unit 7

Sitcom

Cheryl: Hi.
Mother: Hi.
Cheryl: Welcome to my new apartment, Mom!
Mother: I liked your old apartment at 24 Oak Street better.
Cheryl: That's because you live at 22 Oak Street.
Mother: Your old apartment had such a nice view.
Cheryl: The view here is nice too, Mom. The park is just across the street. And my office is around the corner.
Mother: Nice refrigerator. It's very small, isn't it?
Cheryl: The refrigerator?
Mother: The kitchen.
Cheryl: It's a little small, but I like it. There's the dining room, the office, and the living room.
Mother: The chairs are nice. I like the sofa. Why's the dresser in the living room?
Cheryl: There's no place else for it to go.
Mother: But where are the other rooms, honey?
Cheryl: Mom, it's a studio apartment. There are no other rooms.
Mother: This is it?
Cheryl: This is it!
Mother: But where's the bedroom?
Cheryl: Ta da!
Mother: I'm afraid to ask about the bathroom.
Cheryl: Oh, Mom! I think it's nice.

On-the-Street Interviews

Interviewer: Do you live in a house or an apartment?
Rob: I live in an apartment.
Chris: I live in a house.
Christiane: I live in an apartment.
Interviewer: And do you have a large living room?
Catherine: I would say medium-sized.
Interviewer: And what sorts of furniture do you have in your living room?
Rob: We have a sofa and a lounge chair and a coffee table and a television set.
Interviewer: Does your apartment have a lot of windows?
Emma: Actually in every room there's a window.
Interviewer: Does your apartment have a balcony?
Christiane: No, my apartment does not have a balcony.

Interviewer: How about a garden?
Catherine: We do have a backyard.
Interviewer: What appliances are there in your kitchen?
Chris: We've got a cooker, a microwave. We've got a fridge and a freezer, but in fact we've got everything apart from a dishwasher.
Interviewer: And a cooker. What's a cooker?
Chris: A stove.
Interviewer: Do you like your apartment?
Rob: I love my apartment.
Christiane: Yes, I like my apartment a lot.
Interviewer: And why?
Christiane: Because I painted it in my colors, and it's my home and my little castle.

Unit 8

Sitcom

Marie: Paul, you're late again.
Paul: Sorry. I never get up before 8:45.
Marie: 8:45?! That's late!
Paul: What time do you get up?
Marie: 5:00 A.M.
Paul: 5:00 A.M.?! That's early! What do you do in the morning?
Marie: Well, after I get up I usually make breakfast, take out the garbage, do the laundry . . .
Paul: The laundry?
Marie: Yes. Then I read the newspaper, check my e-mail, sometimes I take a nap . . .
Paul: You take a nap in the morning?!
Marie: Just fifteen minutes. On Monday, Wednesday and Friday I exercise. And on the other days I clean the house. Then I take a shower, get dressed, put on my makeup, and go to work.
Paul: Wow. You never sleep late?
Marie: On the weekends I sleep 'til 6:00.
Paul: That's really late. You do laundry in the morning?
Marie: And the evening. Why, when do you do the laundry?
Paul: Usually in March. And September.

On-the-Street Interviews

Interviewer: And could you tell me what you usually do during the week?
Angelique: Usually during the week, um . . ., I mean, I go to a couple of films. I like to go to the movies, independent films.
Interviewer: How often do you do laundry?
Jessica: As little as possible.
Interviewer: Do you take a nap in the afternoon?
Deepti: I don't take a nap in the afternoon. I don't get a chance to.
Interviewer: What time do you usually eat breakfast?
Alvino: Between 6:30 and 7:00.
Interviewer: What time do you usually eat lunch?

Blanche: At noon.

Interviewer: What about dinner. When?

Jessica: Dinner . . . I love to have dinner around 6:00, which is not too late, because if it's too late I can't sleep. So, most of the time around 6:00, 7:00.

Interviewer: So, would you say you're a morning person or an evening person?

Lisa: More of an evening person.

Interviewer: And why do you say that?

Lisa Peters: I think that it takes me a really long time to wake up, so usually anything after 12:00 I'm good to go, and by 7:00 I'm like at full energy.

Unit 9

Sitcom

Marie: What are you doing this weekend? Do you want to go shopping with me?

Cheryl: That sounds great. When do you want to go?

Marie: How about Saturday morning?

Cheryl: I'm making breakfast for some friends at 9:00. Then I'm doing laundry from 11:00 to noon.

Marie: Saturday afternoon?

Cheryl: I'm taking an art class from 1:00 to 3:00. How about 3:30?

Marie: No, I'm exercising with a friend from 3:00 to 4:00. Then I'm going to the movies at 5:00 with my sister.

Cheryl: Sunday morning?

Marie: I'm visiting my parents until 10:00. Then I'm meeting a friend at the art museum until 1:00. Sunday afternoon?

Cheryl: I'm going to a baseball game with Bob at 1:00. How about late afternoon?

Marie: Around 5:00?

Cheryl: Great.

Bob: Hey. Do you want to play basketball tomorrow?

Paul: OK.

On-the-Street Interviews

Interviewer: What are you planning to do this evening?

Joe: This evening I'm planning to go to, um, dinner with friends and maybe some drinks.

Martin: I think I'll stay home and have my dinner.

Interviewer: So what are you going to do this weekend?

San: I am going to go to, um, the park and maybe see a movie and hang out with my friends.

Martin: Um, I'm going to an opera.

Interviewer: That's interesting. And, uh, will you be going with anyone?

Martin: Uh, with a colleague in the office and her husband.

Interviewer: Next month. Do you have any big plans coming up?

Stephan: Um, I don't have major plans coming up next month. I usually go week by week.

San: Next Monday I will, um, probably be in the office working. Um, after work I'll probably go out and, um, have something to eat and go to dinner and, um, come home and watch TV.

Unit 10

Sitcom

Bob: Tonight, I'm cooking.

Cheryl: What are you making?

Bob: Bob's Famous Vegetable Soup. Do you have any vegetables?

Cheryl: I have some onions, tomatoes . . .

Bob: How many tomatoes?

Cheryl: Two. I have some beans, some peas, one cabbage and a potato.

Bob: Great!

Cheryl: You want them all?

Bob: It's vegetable soup. Pass those bananas, please.

Marie: Bananas are fruit.

Bob: Yes.

Marie: You put bananas in your vegetable soup?!

Bob: Sounds good, doesn't it? Now do you have any sugar?

Cheryl: Yes.

Bob: And I need a lemon. Oh, and do you have any coffee?

Cheryl: Do you have a recipe for this?

Bob: Go watch TV, please.

Bob: Come. Have a taste.

Cheryl: This is . . . delicious! Bob, you're a great cook!

Marie: The coffee and bananas are great!

On-the-Street Interviews

Interviewer: Tell me, what beverages do you like to drink?

Ian: Um, coffee, tea, milk, uh, water.

James: Um, I like to drink iced tea—iced tea and water.

Interviewer: How about, um, the foods that you like to eat? Could you tell me some foods that you like to eat?

Dan: Uh, fish and rice.

Interviewer: How often do you eat carrots?

Natalie: I usually eat a salad every day, and in the salad I put carrots.

Interviewer: Do you, um, eat a lot of soup, for example?

James: Yes, a lot of soup.

Dan: Yeah. I have soup occasionally.

Lorayn: In the winter I eat a lot of soup, actually.

Matt: No. I don't eat a lot of soup.

Interviewer: Could you tell me some items that are in your fridge right now?

James: Uh, let's see. Well, we've always got a lot of vegetables because we eat a big salad everyday.

Ian: Uh, bread, cheese, eggs.

Interviewer: What time do you plan to eat lunch today?

Ian: Uh, maybe around three.

Interviewer: So what do you want for dinner tonight?

Lorayn: I would really like sushi for dinner tonight.

Unit 11

Sitcom

Marie: Well, hello, Dr. Anderson! Welcome back.

Dr. Anderson: Thank you very much.

Marie: How was your trip to London?

Dr. Anderson: It was fine, thank you.

Marie: Did you visit lots of museums?

Dr. Anderson: No. I didn't visit any.

Marie: Did you eat in some good restaurants?

Dr. Anderson: No. I ate in the same bad restaurant every day.

Marie: Did you see any plays or concerts?

Dr. Anderson: No. But I watched TV in the hotel room at night.

Marie: Did you take some nice walks around London?

Dr. Anderson: Actually, no. I sat in a chair for four days.

Marie: Dr. Anderson, that doesn't sound like a very nice vacation.

Dr. Anderson: Vacation? I went to London for business, not for vacation. I met doctors from all over the world. We talked about new medicines, and I gave two speeches. I always ate at the hotel restaurant. So I actually never left the hotel.

Marie: But, Dr. Anderson, you were in London and you didn't see the city.

Dr. Anderson: No. But it looked nice from the airplane.

On-the-Street Interviews

Interviewer: What did you do last weekend?

Alvino: I worked.

Rob: Last weekend I went running in the park. I had drinks with friends. I read the paper. I relaxed.

Maiko: I went to see a movie, and, um . . . yes, with my friend, and I went to have some dinner with her.

Interviewer: How about yesterday? What did you do yesterday?

Mauro: Well, yesterday it rained all day in New York, so I just went to the public library.

Interviewer: This past weekend, what was the weather like?

Alvino: It was nice, sunny, pleasant.

Interviewer: Yeah? So you enjoyed it?

Alvino: Yes I did.

Interviewer: You were outside?

Alvino: I was outside working, yes, but enjoying it.

Maiko: It was . . . oh, last weekend it was not too good. Uh, it was rainy, but I think Sunday was pretty good. It was sunny.

Rob: The weather was great.

Interviewer: That sounds really nice.

Rob: It was really nice.

Interviewer: Did you have a good time?

Rob: I did have a good time.

Unit 12

Sitcom

Marie: I'm meeting my sister for lunch.

Cheryl: Aren't you having lunch with Mr. Evans?

Marie: Oh, no! I forgot! Tell him I don't feel well and I'm going to the doctor.

Paul: OK.

Mr. Evans: Is Marie here?

Cheryl: Uh, no. She's not feeling so well.

Bob: She went to the doctor.

Paul: She has a fever. And a headache. And a stomachache. And a toothache.

Mr. Evans: That sounds bad!

Marie: I need my jacket.

Mr. Evans: You do look awful!

Marie: I do?

Mr. Evans: Well, with your fever . . .

Marie: Fever? Oh, yes, fever.

Mr. Evans: And a headache!

Marie: Ohhh!

Mr. Evans: And a stomachache!

Marie: Oooh.

Mr. Evans: And a toothache!

Marie: Ow!!!

Mr. Evans: You're not going anywhere. Stay right here. I'm calling the doctor.

Marie: Yes. Thank you, Mr. Evans. Thank *you* very much.

On-the-Street Interviews

Interviewer: Could you describe your parents for me?

Jessica: My dad is like this tall. He has already white hair, big ears, and is very handsome. And my mom is a little smaller than me, and she has black straight hair and is very beautiful, and has big blue eyes.

Interviewer: Could you tell me what one of your brothers looks like?

Martin: Um, looks like me a little bit. The other one looks more like my mother.

Interviewer: Could you describe them a little bit— their hair, their eyes?

Martin: Uh, they both have black hair and brown eyes, just like me.

Interviewer: Now, do you have any siblings?

Angelique: Yes. I have an older brother.

Interviewer: So is he a handsome guy?

Angelique: I would think so, yes. I think he's very handsome, but he's my brother, so . . .

Interviewer: And how about your sisters? Are they pretty?

Martin: I say they're pretty.

Unit 13

Sitcom

Mr. Evans: Marie, could you do me a favor? I'm having lunch with a client in an hour, and I spilled coffee on my tie. Could you go to the store and buy a new tie for me?

Marie: Sure, no problem.

Mr. Evans: And can you get a newspaper for me at the store on the corner?

Marie: Yup.

Mr. Evans: This coffee is cold. Could you buy me a cup of coffee, too?

Marie: Sure.

Mr. Evans: Also, this shirt doesn't look very nice. Can you buy me a new shirt?

Marie: Of course.

Mr. Evans: Could you get me a new suit, too?

Marie: Yes.

Mr. Evans: And can you play the violin for me after lunch?

Marie: Certainly.

Mr. Evans: Could you fix my car tonight?

Marie: Yes, sir.

Mr. Evans: You didn't hear me at all, did you?

Marie: I'm sorry, what did you say?

Mr. Evans: Nothing. Nothing. I'm going to the store to buy a new tie.

Marie: Okay.

Marie: Can I fix his car tonight? Yeah, right.

On-the-Street Interviews

Interviewer: Tell me a little bit about yourself. Can you play a musical instrument?

Elli: Not at all. I wish I could, but I sing.

Matt: Yes, I can play the guitar.

Interviewer: And when did you learn?

Matt: Um, I started playing the guitar when I was in fifth grade, which is about age eleven, I'd say.

Interviewer: And was it hard to learn?

Matt: Uh, just takes a lot of practice.

Interviewer: Any other musical instruments?

Stephan: I used to play the drums when I was, uh, younger.

San: I cannot play a musical instrument. Um, but I like to dance, so that's kind of related to music.

Interviewer: Can you swim or ski or knit?

Vanessa: Um, I jog. I like to jog. I'm trying to do a marathon, so I've been running. I'm up to five miles. So I run as much as I can every day.

Interviewer: Do you speak any foreign languages?

Stephan: Yes, I do. I speak, uh, five foreign languages.

Interviewer: My goodness. That's a lot. Could you tell me which ones?

Stephan: My native language is Greek, um, and I also speak English, French, Spanish, and Italian.

Interviewer: Can you knit or ski or paint or cook?

San: Yes to a lot of those things. I can cook a little bit. Um, I can ride a bike. I can, um, . . . oh gosh, it's hard to name a lot . . . all the things that you can do when you don't . . . that you take for granted. Um, I can play sports. I can, um, play poker.

Unit 14

Sitcom

Marie: I would like to live in China.

Paul: I'd like to learn to play the guitar.

Marie: If I can't live in China, I'm going to learn to speak Chinese.

Paul: I'm going to write a book.

Marie: Really? About what?

Paul: I don't know. Cooking.

Marie: You don't cook.

Paul: I'll learn.

Marie: What about you two? What are your plans?

Bob: We're going to go to a movie tonight.

Marie: No, what are your plans for the future?

Cheryl: Well, I'd like to get married and have children.

Marie: What about you, Bob?

Bob: I'd like to get married and have children, too.

Marie: Really? You would?

Paul: You want to get married?!

Cheryl: Actually, we have some news for you.

Marie: No! You're getting married?!

Bob: We want you to come to the movie with us.

Marie: Oh.

Bob: And we're going to get married.

Marie: I'm so happy for you!

Paul: Congratulations! Can we still come to the movie with you?

On-the-Street Interviews

Interviewer: So where were you born?

Lorayn: I was born in New York City.

Interviewer: When were you born?

Lorayn: January 28, 1969.

Interviewer: And, uh, did you grow up in New York?

Lorayn: Yes, I did.

Interviewer: Where and what did you study?

Joe: Uh, I studied at, uh, Rutgers, uh, in, uh, New Jersey, and I studied psychology.

Interviewer: What are your future plans?

Christiane: I will work in America and then maybe move to Thailand.

Interviewer: Why do you want to move to Thailand?

Christiane: Because Thailand has beautiful beaches and it's warm all the time.

Interviewer: Do you have any thoughts about getting married? Having children? Raising a family?

Ian: Uh, I'm not up to that yet. No.

Interviewer: Not even thinking about it?

Ian: Well, I'm thinking, I . . . but I'm not up to that yet.

Interviewer: How about, uh, some other thing you might like to do—like learn to play a musical instrument or some other hobby you might like to learn?

Maiko: OK. I really love skiing so, but I'm not too good at it, so, um, I'd love to learn more.

Dan: I'd like to play the violin.

Ian: I'd like to, uh, learn more about writing. I like writing.

Top Notch Pop
Lyrics

Top Notch Pop Lyrics

Excuse Me, Please [Unit 2]

(CHORUS)
Excuse me—please excuse me.
What's your number?
What's your name?
I would love to get to know you,
and I hope you feel the same.

I'll give you my e-mail address.
Write to me at my dot com.
You can send a note in English
so I'll know who it came from.

Excuse me—please excuse me.
Was that 0078?
Well, I think the class is starting,
and I don't want to be late.

But it's really nice to meet you.
I'll be seeing you again.
Just call me on my cell phone
when you're looking for a friend.

(CHORUS)

So welcome to the classroom.
There's a seat right over there.
I'm sorry, but you're sitting in
our teacher's favorite chair!

Excuse me—please excuse me.
What's your number?
What's your name?

Tell Me All about It [Unit 4]

Tell me about your father.
He's a doctor and he's very tall.
And how about your mother?
She's a lawyer. That's her picture on the wall.

Tell me about your brother.
He's an actor, and he's twenty-three.
And how about your sister?
She's an artist. Don't you think she looks like me?

(CHORUS)
Tell me about your family—
who they are and what they do.
Tell me all about it.
It's so nice to talk with you.

Tell me about your family.
I have a brother and a sister, too.
And what about your parents?
Dad's a teacher, and my mother's eyes are blue.

(CHORUS)

Who's the pretty girl in that photograph?
That one's me!
You look so cute!
Oh, that picture makes me laugh!
And who are the people there, right below that one?
Let me see . . . that's my mom and dad.
They both look very young.

(CHORUS)

Tell me all about it.
Tell me all about it.

On the Weekend [Unit 8]

(CHORUS)
On the weekend,
when we go out,
there is always so much joy and laughter.
On the weekend,
we never think about
the days that come before and after.

He gets up every morning.
Without warning, the bedside clock rings the alarm.
So he gets dressed—
he does his best to be on time.
He combs his hair, goes down the stairs,
and makes some breakfast.
A bite to eat, and he feels fine.
Yes, he's on his way
to one more working day.

(CHORUS)

On Thursday night,
when he comes home from work,
he gets undressed, and if his room's a mess,
he cleans the house. Sometimes he takes a rest.
Maybe he cooks something delicious,
and when he's done
he washes all the pots and dishes,
then goes to bed.
He knows the weekend's just ahead.

(CHORUS)

My Favorite Day [Unit 11]

Last night we walked together.
It seems so long ago.
And we just talked and talked.
Where did the time go?

We saw the moonlit ocean
across the sandy beach.
The waves of summer fell,
barely out of reach.

(CHORUS)
Yes, that was then,
and this is now,
and all I do is think about
yesterday,
my favorite day of the week.

When I woke up this morning,
my feelings were so strong.
I put my pen to paper,
and I wrote this song.

I'm glad I got to know you.
You really made me smile.
My heart belonged to you
for a little while.

(CHORUS)

It was wonderful to be with you.
We had so much to say.
It was awful when we waved good-bye.
Why did it end that way?

(CHORUS)

I Wasn't Born Yesterday [Unit 14]

I went to school and learned the lessons
of the human heart.
I got an education in
psychology and art.

It doesn't matter what you say.
I know the silly games you play.

(CHORUS)
I wasn't born yesterday.
I wasn't born yesterday.

Well, pretty soon I graduated
with a good degree.
It took some time to understand
the way you treated me,

and it's too great a price to pay.
I've had enough, and anyway,

(CHORUS)

So you think I'd like to marry you
and be your pretty wife?
Well, that's too bad, I'm sorry, now.
Grow up and get a life!

It doesn't matter what you say.
I know the silly games you play.

(CHORUS)

Answer Key

Answer Key

Unit 1

Preview
A.
1. f **2.** g **3.** a **4.** e **5.** j **6.** i **7.** d **8.** c **9.** b
10. h
B.
2. a **3.** a **4.** an **5.** a **6.** a **7.** an **8.** an **9.** a **10.** a
11. a **12.** a **13.** a **14.** a **15.** an

View
A.
1. Marie **2.** Mr. Rashid **3.** Mr. Evans **4.** Paul **5.** Bob
6. Cheryl
B.
Hi!; It's a pleasure to meet you.; Welcome to Top Notch.;
Nice to meet you.; Glad to meet you.; A pleasure.
C.
1. F **2.** T **3.** F **4.** T **5.** F **6.** F **7.** F **8.** F **9.** F
D.
[Note: both contracted and uncontracted answers are correct.]
1. receptionist **2.** She's; She's; office manager
3. isn't; He isn't; He isn't **4.** He's; He's; tour guide
5. isn't; He's **6.** isn't
E.
1. Are you Bob?
2. Are you an office manager?
3. Is Mr. Evans a tour guide?
4. Are they Bob and Mr. Evans?
G.
Answers will vary but should include variations on the
following:
This is Marie. She's the receptionist at Top Notch Travel.
This is Paul. He's a tour guide.
This is Cheryl. She's the office manager.
This is Bob. He's not the mailman.
This is Mr. Rashid. He's a businessman.

View
A.
1. No, he's not.
2. Yes, she is.
3. No, she's not.
4. No, she's not.
B.
1. b **2.** a **3.** a **4.** c

Unit 2

Preview
A.
2. Vivian's; her **3.** Pam and Ken's; their **4.** Joan's; her
5. Andrew's; his

View
A.
1. b **2.** a **3.** f **4.** e **5.** c **6.** d
B.
1. your friend; a writer
2. Mr. Evans's neighbor; a doctor; an artist
3. our lawyer; not; a musician
4. your boss; That's not
C.
1. are **2.** isn't **3.** is **4.** isn't **5.** is **6.** aren't **7.** is
8. are **9.** isn't
E.
2. This is Nobu Matsuhisa. He's a chef. He's from Japan.
3. This is Frank Gehry. He's an architect. He's from
Canada.
4. This is Paulina Rubio. She's a singer. She's from Mexico.
5. This is Martha Argerich. She's a musician. She's from
Argentina.
6. This is Djimon Hounsou. He's an actor. He's from Benin.

View
A.
1. I'm from; I'm from **2.** are you from; No, I'm not.
B.
1. Deepti; Gupta **2.** 239-0560 **3.** 43 **4.** Fordyce;
ellifordyce@msn.com **5.** 555-1312
C.
1. She's **2.** He's **3.** His **4.** She's **5.** Her
D.
1. Where are you from?
2. What's your name?
3. What's your [cell] phone number?
4. What's your e-mail address?
5. Where are your neighbors from?
6. What's your address?

Top Notch Pop Song
A.
1. number **2.** name **3.** 0078 **4.** your **5.** your
6. What's **7.** What's
B.
1. e-mail address OR dot-com **2.** cell phone
C.
1. a. What's your number? **b.** What's your name?
2. Answers will vary.

Unit 3

Preview

A.
2. It's down the street.
3. It's on the right.
4. It's around the corner.
5. It's on the left.
6. It's across the street.

B.
2. Don't drive; Take 3. Take; Don't take
4. Don't take; Drive 5. Walk; Don't drive

C.
1. Go 2. Turn; Go 3. Go to the corner
4. turn left; one 5. two; right

View

A.
Numbers 1, 2, 6 should be checked.

B.
1. Go to the corner and turn left.
2. Go two blocks and turn right.
3. Don't take the train!
4. Go through the station.

C.
1. b 2. a 3. b

D.
8, 7, 11, 5, 3, 10, 4, 2, 6, 1, 9

E.
Answers will vary but should include variations on the following:
Go to the corner and turn left. Go two blocks and turn right. Go around the corner to the train station. Go through the station. Go across the street to the bookstore. The Red Café is down the street.

View

A.
1. d 2. c 3. a 4. e 5. b
B.
1. c 2. a 3. b 4. c 5. a

Unit 4

Preview

A.
1. b 2. c 3. a 4. a
B.
2. Who are Ann and Joe?
3. Who is Eric?
4. Who is Mark?
5. Who is Katie?
6. Who are Katie and Eric?

C.
1. How old is 2. How old are; is; is 3. How old is; She is/She's 4. How old is Jack's wife? 5. How old are your parents? is; is 6. How old are

View

A.
her brother; her brother's wife; her mother; her sister's husband; her sister's son

B.
2. F; Her brother is **thirty-four**.
3. F; Her mother is **fifty-eight**.
4. F; Her **sister's husband** is an architect.
5. T
6. T

C.
1. a 2. b 3. c 4. b 5. a

D.
1. handsome 2. pretty 3. old 4. cute

E.
1. have; are; is; is 2. has; are; has; has 3. is; is; is; Is; is

View

A.
1. c 2. b 3. c 4. a
B.
1. Who's; I have; children; forty-one; forty-two; forty; thirty-four
2. children; I have two children; son; daughter; are; they're; students

C.
1. F 2. T 3. NI 4. T 5. T 6. F
D.
Answers will vary but may include variations on the following:
1. Her oldest son is forty-one. Her daughter is forty. Her "baby" is thirty-four.
2. Mauro has a son and a daughter. They are students.
3. Chris has a sister. She's twenty-six.
4. Maiko has a brother. He's tall and handsome.

Top Notch Pop Song

A.
doctor, lawyer, actor, artist, teacher
B.
Answers are interchangeable.
2. mother 3. brother 4. sister
C.
1. F 2. T 3. F 4. F 5. F 6. F 7. F

D.
Wording of answers will vary.
1. Yes, he is.
2. She's a lawyer.
3. He's 23.
4. He's an actor.
5. Her sister is an artist.
6. He has one brother and one sister.
7. Her eyes are blue.

Unit 5

Preview

A.
1. T **2.** F **3.** T **4.** T **5.** F **6.** F **7.** T **8.** F **9.** T
10. F
B.
2. Friday and Saturday **3.** 8:30

View

A.
Answers are interchangeable.
1. movie **2.** baseball game **3.** play **4.** concert
5. talk
B.
2. F; Bob's birthday is on Saturday.
3. F; Bob's birthday is on Saturday.
4. F; There's a great French movie at the Avalon.
5. T
6. F; *Life Is a Dream* is a play.
7. T
8. F; There's a Mozart concert on Saturday.
9. T
10. T
C.
1. Cheryl and Bob **2.** Bob **3.** Cheryl; Bob **4.** Bob
5. Cheryl **6.** Cheryl; Bob **7.** Cheryl and Bob
D.
Wording of answers will vary.
1. It's two minutes after six.
2. Bob is two minutes late.
3. Bob's birthday is on Saturday.
4. No. There's a French movie at the Avalon.
5. The baseball game is on Saturday night [at 7:00].
6. The play is at the Arts Center.
7. *Life Is a Dream.*
8. The play is at 8:00 P.M.
9. A Mozart concert is at 7:30 (half past seven).
E.
1. late; What time is it?; after six **2.** Saturday; there's; movie; There's; game; Saturday; there's; play; 8:00 P.M.
3. There's; concert; What time **4.** 7:00; There's a talk; Saturday
F.
1. on; at; at **2.** on; at; in **3.** at; at; in; on **4.** in; at; on
5. at; at; in; on

View

A.
1. Five o'clock **2.** 10:30 **3.** It's 4:15 **4.** ten; to twelve
5. what time is; at six o'clock **6.** what time is it; it is 5:30
7. 29th; September
B.
1. a **2.** a **3.** b **4.** b

Unit 6

Preview

A.
2. a yellow skirt **3.** brown pants **4.** a gray suit
5. a red dress **6.** a purple blouse
B.
2. That; This **3.** Those; These **4.** This; purple; Those; orange **5.** That; clean; These; dirty
C.
1. likes; doesn't like; doesn't like **2.** like; doesn't like; likes **3.** like; don't like; like
D.
1. Do you like **2.** Do; like **3.** Does; like **4.** Does he like

View

A.
The following should be checked: 2, 4, 5, 8, 9.
B.
1. Do you like; blouse; Yes; That; beautiful **2.** these shoes; Do you like; like those shoes; like those shoes
3. this dress; like that; do **4.** this skirt; That skirt; nice
C.
1. What; want **2.** Which; like; likes **3.** wants; does
4. Where do; have **5.** Who needs; does; needs
6. When does

View

A.
1. nice sweater **2.** nice; shirt **3.** That's a really nice tie
4. Do you; black **5.** I like that; Do you like that color
B.
2. Vanessa's blouse is **new**. **3.** Dan **likes** blue.
4. Lorayn **likes** red. **5.** Vanessa's blouse is **green**.
6. San's sweater is **black**. **7. Three** people need new shoes.

Unit 7

Preview

A.
1. bedroom **2.** bathroom **3.** closet **4.** dining room
5. kitchen **6.** living room

B.
1. a bed; a dresser; a table; a lamp; a rug **2.** a sofa; an easy chair; a picture; a TV **3.** a stove; a microwave; a dishwasher; a refrigerator; a freezer **4.** a table; chairs **5.** a toilet; a bathtub; a sink; a shower; a mirror

View

A.
The following should be checked: 1, 2, 3, 4, 5.

B.
1. nice
park; across the street; office; around the corner
2. I like it; dining room; office; living room
3. dresser; living room
There's
4. bathroom

C.
2. Cheryl **likes** the view from her apartment.
3. The park is just **across the street**. / **Cheryl's office** is just around the corner.
4. Cheryl's office is **around the corner**. / The **park** is across the street.
5. Cheryl's mother says the refrigerator is **nice**.
6. Cheryl's mother says the kitchen is **small**.
7. Cheryl's mother **likes** the sofa and the chairs.

View

A.
1. a large living room
2. furniture; have; your living room
We have; sofa; chair; table
3. Does your apartment have a lot of windows
there is a window
4. Does your apartment have a balcony?
does not have
5. your kitchen
microwave; freezer

B.
1. Catherine **2.** Emma **3.** Christiane **4.** Chris
5. Christiane **6.** Chris

C.
1. Rob lives in **an apartment**. / **Chris** lives in a house.
2. **Rob** / **Christiane** / **Emma** lives in an apartment. / **Chris** lives in a house.
3. **Catherine** says she has a medium-sized living room.
4. Rob has **one sofa** / **a sofa** in his living room.
5. **Chris** lives in a house. / Emma lives in **an apartment**.
6. Emma **has** a lot of windows.
7. Christiane's apartment **doesn't have** a balcony.

Unit 8

Preview

A.
1. don't; does
gets up; get up

2. Does; watch
doesn't; do; watch
3. do; go
go to bed; goes to bed
4. do; check
check my e-mail; eat / have / make
5. doesn't; make dinner; makes
6. I don't; does; take

B.
2. We clean the house twice a week.
3. The students check [their] e-mail every day.
4. I do the laundry on Tuesdays.
5. My wife and I exercise four times a week.
6. She takes a shower every day.

C.
2. never **3.** sometimes **4.** usually **5.** never
6. always **7.** always **8.** usually

View

A.
1. 8:45 **2.** 5:00 A.M. **3.** 6:00

B.
make breakfast; take out the garbage; do the laundry; read the newspaper; check her e-mail; take a nap; exercise; clean the house; take a shower; get dressed; put on her makeup; go to work

C.
1. a **2.** b **3.** a **4.** b **5.** c

F.
2. How often does Carla go to concerts?
3. How often does Louis sleep late?
4. How often do Pat and Bill run in the park?
5. How often does Victor walk to work?
6. How often does Frank play soccer?
7. How often do Bob and Beth do the laundry?

View

A.
1. e **2.** d **3.** a **4.** b **5.** c **6.** f

B.
1. Jessica **2.** Alvino **3.** Angelique **4.** Deepti

C.
1. Usually; go; like; go **2.** take a nap **3.** have dinner; late; late

Top Notch Pop Song

A.
1. go out **2.** come **3.** gets up **4.** gets dressed
5. combs **6.** makes **7.** go out **8.** come **9.** comes home **10.** gets undressed **11.** cleans **12.** cooks
13. washes **14.** goes to bed **15.** go out **16.** come

B.
Answers can include: gets dressed, combs his hair, goes down the stairs, makes breakfast, eats breakfast, goes to work

C.

Answers can include: gets undressed, cleans the house, takes a rest [or nap], cooks [dinner], washes [all the pots and] the dishes, goes to bed

Unit 9

Preview

A.

1. a **2.** c **3.** b **4.** a **5.** c **6.** b **7.** b

B.

1. are making **2.** are; doing **3.** is; eating **4.** is talking
5. are; meeting

View

A.

1. morning
I'm making
2. I'm exercising; I'm going; my sister
3. morning
I'm visiting; parents; 10:00
4. afternoon
I'm going; game; Bob

B.

1. c **2.** a **3.** b **4.** b **5.** a **6.** c

C.

2. Marie's exercising with a friend on Saturday afternoon.
3. Cheryl's taking an art class from 1:00 to 3:00 on Saturday.
4. Marie's meeting a friend at the art museum on Sunday morning.
5. Cheryl's going to a baseball game with Bob on Sunday afternoon.
6. Marie and her sister are going to the movies on Saturday afternoon at 5:00. / Cheryl and Marie are going shopping on Sunday afternoon at around 5:00.

View

A.

1. What are you; this evening
This evening; with friends
2. this weekend
the park; a movie; hang out with my friends
3. a colleague; office; husband
4. Do you have
I don't have; next month

B.

1. b **2.** a **3.** b **4.** a **5.** c

C.

Answers will vary. Possibilities include:
2. Martin's staying home and having dinner this evening.
3. Martin's going to an opera this weekend.
4. San's going to the park, seeing a movie, and hanging out with her friends this weekend.
5. San's working next Monday.

Unit 10

Preview

A.

2. How many; are there
There are three
3. Are there any
Yes, there are
4. How many; are there
There are five
5. Are there any
No, there aren't
6. How many; are there
There aren't any
7. How many; are there
There are four

B.

1. a can of **2.** a bag of **3.** a box of **4.** a bottle of
5. a loaf of

C.

1. How many; onions; are there
2. How much; tea; is there
3. Is there any; coffee
4. How many; potatoes; are there
5. Are there any; beans
6. How much; juice; is there
7. How much; salt; is there
8. Is there any; bread

View

A.

onions; tomatoes; beans; peas; cabbage; a potato; bananas; sugar; a lemon; coffee

B.

2. **Cheryl** has fruits and vegetables in her fridge.
3. There are **two** tomatoes in the fridge.
4. Cheryl **has** sugar.
5. Bob wants **a lemon**.
6. There **are two cans** of soup on the counter.
7. Marie and Cheryl **like** Bob's soup.
8. Marie **likes** the bananas and coffee in Bob's soup.

C.

1. Do you have
onions, tomatoes
How many tomatoes
Two; beans; peas; cabbage; a potato
2. bananas; soup
do you have; sugar
3. need a lemon; coffee
Go watch TV

F.

1. is making **2.** is mixing **3.** is putting **4.** is opening

G.

Answers to questions will vary.
1. put **2.** eat **3.** cook **4.** sprinkle **5.** drink

View

A.
1. f, b, c, d
2. b, d
3. a, e

B.
1. usually eats **2.** usually eats **3.** sometimes eats
4. doesn't usually eat

C.
1. vegetables **2.** cheese, eggs, bread **3.** 3:00
4. dinner

Unit 11

Preview

A.
2. Who **wanted** the newspaper?
3. When **did** you take vacation?
4. Where **was** the movie?
5. How **did** you get there?
6. They **weren't** late; they **were** early.
7. We **liked** that restaurant.
8. **Did** the house have three bedrooms? Yes, it **did**.
9. Who **had** brown shoes?
10. It **was** a great movie. I **loved** it.

View

A.
1. T **2.** F **3.** F **4.** F **5.** T **6.** F **7.** T **8.** F

B.
1. How was **2.** It was **3.** Did **4.** visit **5.** didn't visit
6. Did **7.** eat **8.** ate **9.** Did **10.** see **11.** watched
12. Did **13.** take **14.** sat

C.
Answers will vary but should include variations on the
following:
She ate in the same bad restaurant every day.
She sat in a chair for four days.
She met doctors from all over the world.
She talked about new medicines.
She gave two speeches.

D.
Answers will vary but should include variations on the
following:
She didn't visit any museums.
She didn't eat in any good restaurants.
She didn't see any plays or concerts.
She didn't take any walks.
She didn't leave the hotel.

View

A.
a. went **b.** worked **c.** read **d.** relaxed **e.** had
f. went **g.** went **h.** had
1. c, d, g, h

2. a, e
3. f
4. b

B.
1. What did you do
worked
went running; park
2. weekend; what was
nice; sunny
weekend; was not; it was; Sunday was; It was sunny

Top Notch Pop Song

A.
1. T **2.** F **3.** T **4.** F **5.** T **6.** T **7.** T

B.
1. walked **2.** talked **3.** talked **4.** did; go **5.** saw
6. was **7.** woke up **8.** were **9.** wrote **10.** got
11. made **12.** was **13.** was **14.** had **15.** was

Unit 12

Preview

B.
1. long; wavy **2.** dark; straight **3.** long; blonde
4. curly; black **5.** Answers will vary.

C.
2. Her eyes are brown.
3. His hair is long and dark.
4. Her eyelashes are long and blonde.
5. Her hair is curly and red.
6. His eyes are green.
7. Her hair is wavy and white.
8. His hair is long and straight.

View

A.
3, 6, 8, 9

B.
1. F **2.** F **3.** F **4.** F **5.** T

C.
1. m meeting my sister
having lunch
2. Is Marie here?
went to the doctor.
3. has a fever; a headache; a stomachache; a toothache
bad
4. I need my
awful

View

A.
1. c **2.** d **3.** b

B.
1. father; He; ears; white **2.** mother; She; straight; blue
3. brothers; black; brown **4.** sisters **5.** brother

C.

1. your parents
   tall
2. your brothers
   like me
   hair; eyes
   black; brown
3. your sisters; pretty
   pretty

Unit 13

A.

2. Could you / Can you; take out
3. Could you / Can you; come
4. Could you / Can you; turn off
5. Could you / Can you; close

View

A.

3, 7, 6, 1, 2, 4, 5

B.

1. a   2. b   3. a   4. a   5. b   6. c

C.

1. Could you   2. a new tie   3. Sure, no problem
4. can you   5. newspaper   6. Yup   7. coffee   8. cold
9. Could you   10. coffee   11. Sure   12. shirt   13. nice
14. Can you   15. shirt   16. Of course   17. Could you
18. new suit   19. Yes   20. Can you   21. after lunch
22. Certainly   23. Could you fix my car   24. Yes, sir

D.

buy coffee for him; get a newspaper

View

A.

1. Elli   2. Matt   3. Stephan   4. Vanessa   5. San
6. Stephan   7. San

B.

1. Can; play
   could; sing
   cannot play; dance
2. Yes, I do; five
3. knit; ski; paint
   can cook; can; a bike

Unit 14

Preview

B.

1. I am going to see a dentist this morning
2. We are going to have a baby in April
3. My brother is going to graduate in May
4. Where are they going to study psychology
5. Who is going to make dinner tonight
6. When are you going to go on vacation

View

A.

1. d   2. b   3. f   4. c   5. a   6. e

B.

1. T   2. T   3. T   4. F   5. F   6. T

C.

1. I can't live in China; m going to learn; Chinese; write a book; I don't know
2. You would; get married; we have; for you; You're getting married; We want; come to the movie; we're going to get married

View

A.

1. Lorayn   2. Christiane   3. Joe   4. Ian   5. Maiko
6. Dan

B.

1. F   2. T   3. F   4. T   5. F

C.

1. where were you born; was born; when were you born; did you grow up
2. what did you; studied; studied psychology
3. are your; work; move; do you want to move; it's warm

E.

1. have   2. are going to go   3. get   4. visit   5. studies

Top Notch Pop Song

A.

1. went   2. learned   3. got   4. psychology   5. wasn't
6. wasn't   7. graduated   8. wasn't   9. wasn't   10. I'd
like to   11. Grow up   12. wasn't   13. wasn't

B.

1. F   2. T   3. T   4. T   5. F